Cheating Academic Integrity
integrity research and practice over the past thirty years from a variety of global perspectives and prepares us for what to expect in the coming decades. This book is essential reading for academic integrity scholars, administrators, and higher education professionals.

—Sarah Elaine Eaton, University of Calgary

This is a must read for all those who want to develop effective data-informed academic integrity policies. *Cheating Academic Integrity* provides practical advice with a thorough review of the literature, written by leading experts in the field who answer questions from why students choose to cheat, how has technology impacted the availability of information and the detection of cheating, how our academic policies on this issue can lead to inequities, and how to reconsider a teaching and learning focus when developing strategies, pedagogies, and assessments that lead to a mindset that promotes academic integrity on your campus.

—Beth M. Schwartz, Provost – Endicott College

Cheating Academic Integrity

Cheating Academic Integrity

LESSONS FROM 30 YEARS
OF RESEARCH

David A. Rettinger
Tricia Bertram Gallant

WILEY

Jossey-Bass
A Wiley Imprint
111 River St, Hoboken, NJ 07030
www.josseybass.com

Simultaneously published in Canada

Jossey-Bass books and products are available through most bookstores. To contact Jossey-Bass directly, call our Customer Care Department within the U.S. at 800–956–7739, outside the U.S. at +1 317 572 3986, or fax +1 317 572 4002.

Wiley also publishes its books in a variety of electronic formats and by print-on-demand. Some material included with standard print versions of this book may not be included in e-books or in print-on-demand. If this book refers to media such as a CD or DVD that is not included in the version you purchased, you may download this material at http://booksupport.wiley.com. For more information about Wiley products, visit www.wiley.com.

Library of Congress Cataloging-in-Publication Data

Names: Rettinger, David A., author. | Bertram Gallant, Tricia, 1970– author.
Title: Cheating academic integrity : lessons from 30 years of research / David A. Rettinger, Tricia Bertram Gallant.
Description: First Edition. | Hoboken, NJ : Jossey-Bass, [2022] | Includes index.
Identifiers: LCCN 2021061618 (print) | LCCN 2021061619 (ebook) | ISBN 9781119868170 (Paperback) | ISBN 9781119868194 (Adobe PDF) | ISBN 9781119868187 (ePub)
Subjects: LCSH: Cheating (Education) | College teaching—Moral and ethical aspects. | College students—Conduct of life.
Classification: LCC LB3609 .R47 2022 (print) | LCC LB3609 (ebook) | DDC 808.02/5—dc23/eng/20220217
LC record available at https://lccn.loc.gov/2021061618
LC ebook record available at https://lccn.loc.gov/2021061619

COVER DESIGN: PAUL MCCARTHY
COVER ART: © GETTY IMAGES | MOHD HAFIEZ MOHD RAZALI / EYEEM

FIRST EDITION

SKY10033201_030122

*To Donald L. McCabe and the other founders of
the International Center for Academic Integrity*

Contents

CONTENTS

List of Authors

Anderman, Eric M.
The Ohio State University

Bertram Gallant, Tricia
University of California, San Diego

Black, Arianna
The Ohio State University

Carson, Mariko L.
Howard University

Cullen, Courtney
University of Georgia

Curtis, Guy J.
University of Western Australia

Dahl, Audun
University of California, Santa Cruz

Goldman, Jacqueline A.
Oregon State University

Harrison, Douglas
University of Maryland, Global Campus

Ives, Robert T.
University of Nevada, Reno

Lancaster, Thomas
Imperial College London

Perry, Andrew H.
The Ohio State University

Rettinger, David A.
University of Mary Washington

Rogerson, Ann M.
University of Wollongong

Simonds, Jennifer
University of Maryland, Global Campus

Spencer, Sharon
University of Maryland, Global Campus

LIST OF AUTHORS

Tilak, Shantanu
The Ohio State University
von Spiegel, Jacqueline
The Ohio State University

Waltzer, Talia
University of California, Santa
Cruz

CHAPTER 1

Cheating Academic Integrity: Lessons from 30 Years of Research

Tricia Bertram Gallant[1] and David A. Rettinger[2]

[1]University of California, San Diego
[2]University of Mary Washington

To cheat means to "act dishonestly or unfairly in order to gain an advantage" (Oxford Languages). Most readers will bristle at the thought of being lied to or being treated unfairly. This bristle instinct seems to be biological. In 2003, Brosnan and de Waal published a study in *Nature* showing that capuchin monkeys are exquisitely sensitive to unfairness, including the famous video of one experimental subject throwing cucumbers at the experimenter after witnessing an unfairly generous reward of grapes to another monkey. So, while it seems clear that both humans and monkeys detest unfairness, cheating in school persists. How can this be the case?

Stephens (2019) argued that cheating persists because it is natural and normal; that is, the propensity to cheat (deceive or trick), despite our instinct to avoid unfairness, was developed as a method for survival. This evolutionary development is even exemplified in our contemporary colloquial language such as in the English phrase "cheating death".

It is within this vein that this book is written. The authors in this book illustrate not only how students cheat academic integrity by their decisions, choices and behaviors but also how instructors and higher education institutions cheat academic integrity by *their* decisions, choices and behaviors. In other words, through this book, we will learn that cheating occurs because of them (the students) and because of us (the faculty and staff).

It is imperative that we, as educators, understand the complex relationship between forces that can serve either to cheat academic integrity or to promote and support it. While cheating may be normal and natural, it is still "unethical and evitable" (Stephens, 2019). It is unethical because left unaddressed, cheating creates tears in the fabric of higher education. Cheating undermines raison dêtre, which can be stated simply as facilitating, assessing, and certifying learning. Given the essential role that higher education plays in twenty-first century economics, democracy, health and sustainability, we cannot afford to idly watch the fabric be torn or participate in the tearing ourselves. The good news is that there is no need to do so. The last 30 years of research has taught us that cheating is evitable; we can do things to mitigate and minimize it.

This book, along with its companion piece (a special issue of the *Journal of College and Character*, volume 23(1), published in February 2022), illuminates a positive way forward that is not only good for our students but also for our shared goals of growing and certifying knowledge as well as developing ethical citizens and professionals. Both this volume and the special issue were created to celebrate and learn from 30 years of research on academic integrity, a research agenda that can be largely credited to the initial research agenda of Donald McCabe and the formation of the International Center for Academic Integrity (ICAI) in 1992. Together, these two volumes provide researchers, instructors, staff, and administrators with a scholarly perspective on the causes and context of cheating as well as the internal and external factors that serve to either promote and support academic integrity or to cheat academic integrity.

INTRODUCTION OF EACH CHAPTER

The last 30 years of research on academic integrity was vast, so we start at the beginning with two chapters that look at what we know about the prevalence of cheating during this time. First, in *Trends in Plagiarism and Cheating Prevalence*, Curtis makes an important declaration that may surprise our readers: The prevalence of cheating and plagiarism may have decreased, not increased, over the last 30 years. Curtis posits this may be a result of an increase in preventative measures taken by higher education institutions to enhance awareness of honor and integrity as well as skills in writing with integrity. Despite this good news, though, Curtis warns us that there are threats to integrity not yet realized, including rippling effects of the COVID pandemic and emerging technologies that will require substantive changes to forms of assessment less we be assessing how well machines, rather than our students, are demonstrating knowledge and abilities.

Lancaster picks up on Curtis' idea of "rippling effects" in his piece on contract cheating. Lancaster notes that while the term contract cheating was coined in 2006 and the behavior (arranging for someone else to complete your academic work) existed long before then, the explosion of research on contract cheating really did not occur until 2017. Since that time, our understanding of contract cheating has expanded exponentially. We now know, for example, that friends and families are the most likely providers of contract cheating services, and that remote instruction substantially increased the use of commercial contract cheating providers, especially amongst those that brand themselves as legitimate "homework help sites". Lancaster foreshadows the challenging road ahead for academic integrity with the emerging technologies, such as automated writing and problem solving programs achievable through artificial intelligence. Like Curtis, Lancaster suggests that we must approach education very differently now and in the future from a learning perspective, but Lancaster also adds from a cybersecurity or safety perspective.

So, why are we here, still worrying about cheating and threats to the integrity of the academic enterprise after 30 years of research and hundreds of years of practice? The next two chapters try to answer that question.

First, readers are drawn into the psychological research on cheating as explored by Anderman and colleagues, particularly the research into academic motivation and academic integrity. This chapter reminds us that cheating is rather natural, a normal and expected phenomenon brought on by individual human factors like how and to what we attribute the cause of events (attribution theory), how our goal orientations influence our behaviors (achievement goal theory), how our behaviors are also shaped by what we see happening around us in our environment and by our peers (social-cognitive theory), how our expectations for success or self-efficacy influence our choices and behaviors (Situated Expectancy-Value Theory), and finally, how our needs for autonomy, competence and belonging may dictate how we respond when these need resolution is frustrated (self-determination theory). Anderman and colleagues' review of the research educates us that while these theories explain why cheating is a normal outgrowth of education and development, the research and theories also help us identify solutions to minimize cheating and enhance integrity and learning. Readers interested in crafting their own research agendas to explore academic motivation and academic integrity are provided suggestions for moving the knowledge forward, and those interested in evolving their own teaching to enhance academic integrity may pick and choose from the nine practical suggestions offered in the chapter.

Next, Waltzer and Dahl use insights from psychological theories and research to posit a bold new hypothesis that students do perceive cheating as "wrong", and they act in concordance with this moral judgement the majority of the time. However, when students do cheat, which the authors argue is rare, it happens for one of three psychological causes: 1) students perceive the behavior incorrectly based on the facts available to them; 2) students evaluate the act as cheating but still consider it a better option than an alternative; or 3) students decide the act is cheating but yet acceptable in some circumstances. Waltzer and Dahl use the literature of the last 30 years to level out support for their hypothesis as well as to suggest the resulting implications for research and practice. For example, when do students see cheating as acceptable or not? Do notions of cheating develop or change over time? What types of interventions could be designed to simultaneously target student perceptions, evaluations, and decisions about cheating? Which interventions—in the moment of the cheating decision—might be most effective in enhancing integrity?

This last question provides the perfect segue into the next chapter by Goldman, Carson and Simonds who focus on evidence-based pedagogical practices to promote academic integrity and thus prevent cheating. Goldman and colleagues suggest that the complex interplay of forces shaping cheating can be best addressed not by surveillance or other forms of policing student conduct but by choosing and implementing high-impact pedagogical practices. Such practices like problem-based learning and service learning, not only engage and motivate students in their own learning but they help create a sense of belonging, meet students where they are at in their own lived experiences, and generate an inclusive classroom environment in which academic integrity will be more normative than cheating.

The idea that better pedagogy can address many of the causes of cheating is picked up in the next chapter by Harrison and Spencer, who focus on what we've learned about the relationship between pedagogy and cheating as a result of the pandemic and the abrupt move to Emergency Remote Teaching (ERT). After cogently arguing that ERT is not equivalent to online learning, Harrison and Spencer walk us through what the last 30 years have taught us about academic integrity and online learning. Particularly that we should not expect to combat cheating with blunt force objects like surveillance technology; we have seen during the pandemic era the many downsides of such a reliance. Instead, we should be embracing the good pedagogical techniques that we know work for enhancing learning and integrity regardless of instructional modality: 1) cultivating and maintaining socially presence, a sense of community, and social engagement if you will; 2) building and supporting cognitive presence, the purposeful intellectual engagement in the learning activities; and, 3) universally designing learning experiences to meet the full range of diversity that is in the classroom.

After this thorough exploration in six different chapters of the state of cheating in the twenty-first century, as well as the causes and solutions for cheating, the authors of the next chapter wrap it up in a bow of sorts with a review of the most influential writings on academic integrity of the last 30 years. In 2012, the International Center for Academic Integrity (ICAI) celebrated its twentieth anniversary by selecting and publishing an AI Reader which listed the 43 pieces of academic writing that were most influential in shaping research and practice. In 2022, ICAI is celebrating its thirtieth anniversary and has, once again, selected the most influential pieces written on academic integrity between 2010–2020. Rogerson, Bertram Gallant, Cullen and Ives explore these 80+ pieces to call out the themes that seem to drive the research agenda, the lessons that have informed practice, and the ways in which research influenced, and were influenced by, cultural and contextual factors prevalent at the time. From this chapter, readers will be able to envision the next 30 years of an academic integrity research agenda along with the areas of practice on which we should be focusing now and into the future.

CONCLUSION

In the past 30 years, cheating in school has moved in and out of the periphery of the public eye, but the abrupt move to (and then lingering of) Emergency Remote Teaching (ERT) and the explosion of new educationally-peripheral technologies (e.g. proctoring companies; contract cheating providers), served to bring academic cheating into sharp focus for both the industry press (e.g. Lederman, 2020; Supiano, 2020) and general interest news media (CBS News, 2021; Hobbs, 2021; Moody, 2021; Newton, 2020). Higher education is at a crossroads and after the "Varsity Blues" scandal (Medina, Benner, and Taylor, 2019), the public is questioning the fairness of the education system as a whole. Cheating can tear at the fabric of the entire enterprise of higher education by turning any university into a diploma mill, so it has never been more important to ensure that students are graduating with an authentic education that prepares them for life as a whole human.

Together, the chapters is this book, and its companion piece (*Journal of College and Character*, 23(1), 2022), provide researchers, instructors, students, and staff with 30 years of knowledge about how we can all do more to stop cheating academic integrity and to start prioritizing the integrity of the academic experience and the academic degree in the twenty-first century. Readers who have not yet found the special journal issue should add it to their reading list because it includes topics not covered explicitly in this volume, such as the influence of research from the Australasia region on our understandings of cheating; the important policy and procedure features that institutions must consider, including the history and impact of honor codes; the evolution in universities from punitive to educational responses to cheating; and finally, the call for institutions to attend to the complexities and needs of our student populations who come to higher education with linguistic and cultural diversities that impact how they relate and experience learning, academic work, and academic integrity.

REFERENCES

CBS News (2021).'As online education grows, the business of cheating is booming'. Available at: **https://www.cbsnews.com/news/ online-education-cheating-business/** (Accessed: November 15, 2021).

Hobbs, T.D. (2021). 'Cheating at school is easier than ever—and it's rampant', *The Wall Street Journal*, 12 May. Available at: **https://www.wsj.com/articles/cheating-at-school-is-easier-than-everand-its-rampant-11620828004** (Accessed: November 15, 2021).

Lederman, D. (2020). 'Best way to stop cheating in online courses? "Teach better"', *Inside Higher Education*. Available at: **https://www.insidehighered.com/digital-learning/article/2020/07/22/technology-best-way-stop-online-cheating-no-experts-say-better** (Accessed: November 15, 2021).

Medina, J., Benner, K., and Taylor, K. (2019). 'Actresses, business leaders and other wealthy parents charged in US college entry fraud', *The New York Times*, 12 March. Available at: **https://www.nytimes.com/2019/03/12/us/college-admissions-cheating-scandal.html** (Accessed: November 15, 2021).

Moody, J. (2021). 'How cheating in college hurts students', *US News*, 31 March. Available at: **https://www.usnews.com/education/best-colleges/articles/how-cheating-in-college-hurts-students** (Accessed: November 15, 2021).

Newton, D. (2020). 'Another program with shifting education online: cheating', *The Hechinger Report,* August 7. Available at: **https://hechingerreport.org/another-problem-with-shifting-education-online-cheating/** (Accessed: November 15, 2021).

Stephens, J.M. (2019). 'Natural and normal, but unethical and evitable: The epidemic of academic dishonesty and how we end it', *Change: The Magazine of Higher Learning*, 51(4), pp. 8–17.

Supiano, B. (2020). 'Students cheat. How much does it matter?', *The Chronicle of Higher Education*, October 21. Available at: **https://www.chronicle.com/article/students-cheat-how-much-does-it-matter** (Accessed: November 15, 2021).

CHAPTER 2

Trends in Plagiarism and Cheating Prevalence: 1990–2020 and Beyond

Guy J. Curtis

University of Western Australia, School of Psychological Science

It is easy to find assertions in the media that both plagiarism (Matthews, 2020) and cheating (Guessoum, 2021) are run-away epidemics. I often encounter articles on cheating or plagiarism that begin with an assertion that academic misconduct is on the rise. Such an opening to an article is a great way to make this point: Academic misconduct is a growing problem that needs to be addressed right now! However, it is important to ask whether this point is, in fact, true.

In this chapter, I discuss the trends in the prevalence of plagiarism and cheating in the past 30 years (1990–2020). Faculty, administrators, and other higher education professionals need to know how much plagiarism and cheating is happening in order to know what they can do to combat academic misconduct. Knowing how prevalent academic misconduct is and how this prevalence may be changing can help higher education institutions get ahead of this problem and act, preemptively, to prevent it.

This chapter begins with a review of three studies that conducted repeated surveys, at different points in time, using the same measures and with similar student groups. These *time-lag studies of plagiarism and cheating* suggest that the prevalence of self-reported academic misconduct has trended downward over the period from 1990 to 2020. Next, I consider whether the downward trend in plagiarism and cheating may be accounted for by students switching to newer forms of misconduct. Specifically, I examine *trends in the prevalence of self-reported commercial contract cheating* from 1990 to 2020. Despite moral panic over commercial contract cheating (Walker and Townley, 2012), there does not appear to be an upward historical trend in its prevalence in this period that would account for a reduction in other forms of plagiarism and cheating. Subsequently, I review studies of *intervention-related change in academic misconduct*, which suggest that educational, technological, and policy developments may account for the downward trend in academic misconduct. Finally, I discuss *current and future threats to academic integrity* that may influence the future prevalence of academic misconduct.

TIME-LAG STUDIES OF PLAGIARISM AND CHEATING

Within the academic integrity literature, many studies can provide a one-off estimate of plagiarism and cheating prevalence at a single point in time. Some studies have specifically investigated the prevalence of academic misconduct by students (e.g. Lim and See, 2001), while others incidentally provide an estimate of misconduct prevalence in studies examining other issues such as predictors of cheating (e.g. Roig and Caso, 2005). Such studies could be used to map historical trends in plagiarism and cheating prevalence over the past 30 years. However, the great diversity of samples, methods, and measures in these studies means that comparison of any one study with another is a comparison of an apple with an orange. Take, for example, two studies conducted in 2015: Abukari (2016) found that 45.8 percent of a sample of 488 Ghanaian students paid someone else to do their homework; in contrast, Roth (2017) found that 0.9 percent of nearly 5,000 American students bought or sold assessment work or study materials. These studies each provide a prevalence estimate of homework outsourcing and sharing where one is more than 50 times higher than the other. These differences may be attributable to the different cultural contexts, samples, and questions that students were asked.

McCabe et al. (2012) sum up concerns about, and causes for, the striking differences in estimates of cheating and plagiarism prevalence that come from dissimilar studies:

> [S]ignificant disparities exist in research estimates of the percentage of college students who engage in academic dishonesty, ranging from 3% (Karlins et al., 1988) to 98% (Gardner et al., 1988). These discrepancies largely stem from differences in research methodology, including research design (e.g. survey vs. experiment), how cheating is defined and operationalized (e.g. self-reports vs. observed or actual cheating), and the time frame examined. (p. 37)

Thus, to most accurately chart historical trends, the most valid data come from studies that have examined similar samples of students using the same measures repeatedly over time. However, not all studies with a longitudinal focus on academic misconduct measure the prevalence of plagiarism and cheating (e.g. Macale et al., 2017; Molnar, 2015). Additionally, repeated sampling over time should ideally be from surveys conducted more than twice in order to assess trends—as Curtis and Vardanega (2016) quipped "two data points do not make a trend, they make a line" (p. 1170). Remarkably, only three research programs in the last 30 years have collected data consistently, from similar college student samples that allow for a like-with-like comparison of general trends in the prevalence of plagiarism and cheating with more than two times of testing.

Strictly speaking, a longitudinal research design collects data from the same people on more than one occasion (Hartmann, 1992). Importantly, longitudinal studies of student cheating over decades are impossible to conduct because students typically pass through their higher education studies from commencement to graduation within a period of three to six years before entering the workforce. As Curtis and Vardanega (2016) point out, studying similar cohort groups of people at multiple points in time is a time-lag, rather than a longitudinal, study. Therefore, to look at prevalence trends from 1990–2020, we must look at the three research programs that have used time-lag designs.

For convenience, I will refer to the three programs of research that have conducted time-lag studies of plagiarism and cheating prevalence by the most recent publications of their data: Stiles et al. (2018), McCabe et al. (2012), and Curtis and Tremayne (2021). The studies incorporated within these publications, their

Table 1 Details of the three time-lag studies of plagiarism and cheating 1990–2020

Most recent report of the study	Stiles et al. (2018)	McCabe et al. (2012)	Curtis and Tremayne (2021)
Previous incremental reports of the study	Vandehey et al. (2007), Diekhoff et al. (1996)	McCabe and Trevino (1993), McCabe and Trevino (1997), McCabe et al. (2001)	Curtis and Vardanega (2016), Curtis and Popal (2011), Maxwell et al. (2006)
Years of data collection and number (n) of students	1994 ($n = 474$) 2004 ($n = 401$) 2014 ($n = 506$)	1990/91 ($n = 2,854$) 1993/94 ($n = 1,744$) 1999/2000 ($n = 693$) 2002–2012 ($n = 73,738$)	2004 ($n = 425$) 2009 ($n = 119$) 2014 ($n = 106$) 2019 ($n = 1099$)

data collection years, and the number of students who completed survey measures are summarized in Table 1.

Next, I outline the methodologies of these studies. Then a graph is presented summarizing the aggregate percentages of students who engaged in any form of plagiarism or cheating at least once over time. In all cases, these studies collected self-report data from college students. One common methodological evolution in each of the three studies was a transition from pencil-and-paper to online survey data collection as technology progressed.

Stiles et al. (2018)

The studies of Stiles et al. (2018) commenced with Haines et al.'s (1986) study in 1984 and used a questionnaire developed for that study. All survey participants were undergraduate students at Midwestern State University in Texas. Students in these studies answered the three questions listed below (1–3) using a response scale to indicate their frequency of ever cheating:

1. Have you ever cheated on a major exam?
2. Have you ever cheated on a daily or weekly quiz?
3. Have you ever cheated on a class assignment (i.e. term paper, lab assignment, homework assignment, etc.)?

A fourth item, "Have you ever helped someone else cheat?" was added in the 2014 survey. Cheating was measured on a 0 to 4 scale from low to high cheating, where 0 was "no," and 1 or higher was coded as "yes". Students who had ever engaged in any of the cheating behaviors listed above were counted as having cheated in order to estimate the total prevalence of cheating in each survey.

McCabe et al. (2012)

McCabe and colleagues' work surveyed large groups of undergraduate and graduate students over multiple institutions and campuses. Some of the same institutions made the survey available to their students in several of the years in which data were collected. Students in these studies indicated their engagement in numerous types of cheating and plagiarism behaviors within the last year, based on Bowers's (1964) study, with nine behaviors (below) common across all times of testing.

1. Copying a few sentences of material without footnoting in a paper.
2. "Padding" a few items on a bibliography.
3. Plagiarized from public material on papers.
4. Getting questions or answers from someone who has already taken the same exam.
5. Copying from another student on a test or exam.
6. Working on the same homework with several students when the teacher doesn't allow it.
7. Turned in papers done entirely, or in part, by other students.
8. Giving answers to other students during an exam.
9. Used crib notes during an exam.

Students who had ever engaged in any of the behaviors listed above were counted as having cheated/plagiarized to estimate the total prevalence of cheating/plagiarism in each survey.

Curtis and Tremayne (2021)

Curtis and Tremayne's (2021) studies were conducted at Western Sydney University, previously named the University of Western Sydney until 2015, and most participants were undergraduate students from this university, with some graduate students also surveyed. Students in these studies were presented with scenarios representing seven forms for plagiarism as defined by Walker (1998); see Table 2 (see also Maxwell et al., 2008).

Students were asked how frequently they had ever engaged in the behaviors described in each scenario using a 5-point scale

Table 2 Types of plagiarism

Type	Definition
Sham Paraphrasing	Material copied verbatim from text and source acknowledged in-line but represented as paraphrased.
Illicit Paraphrasing	Material paraphrased from text without in-line acknowledgement of source
Other Plagiarism	Material copied from another student's assignment with the knowledge of the other student
Verbatim Copying	Material copied verbatim from text without in-line acknowledgement of the source
Recycling	Same assignment submitted more than once for different courses
Ghost Writing	Assignment written by a third party and represented as own work
Purloining	Assignment copied from another student's assignment or other person's papers without that person's knowledge

Note: From Walker, J. (1998). 'Student Plagiarism in Universities: What Are We Doing About It?', *Higher Education Research and Development, 17,* p. 103. Copyright © HERDSA, reprinted by permission of Taylor and Francis Ltd.

from 1 "never" through a range of frequencies to 5 "more than 7 times". Students who had ever engaged in any of the plagiarism or cheating behaviors described in the scenarios were counted as having plagiarized/cheated to estimate the total prevalence of plagiarism/cheating in each survey.

Trends from the time-lag studies

As you can see in Figure 1, the first two surveys from McCabe et al. (2012) in the early 1990s are the only hint of any increase

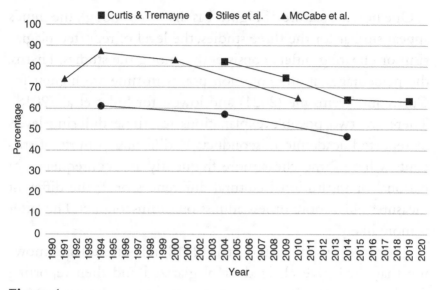

Figure 1

Note: Curtis and Tremayne (2021)—any of 7 forms of plagiarism at least once, McCabe et al. (2012)—any of 9 cheating behaviors at least once, Stiles et al. (2018)—any affirmative response on 3-4-item cheating survey.

in the percentage of students engaging in cheating or plagiarism; otherwise, the trend in the three lines on the graph is consistently downward over time. Indeed, the difference between more recent prevalence rates and older prevalence rates is statistically significant within all three studies.

There are three years in common in which data were collected among the three time-lag studies: 1994 (McCabe et al., 2012 and Stiles et al., 2018), 2004, and 2014 (Curtis and Tremayne, 2021 and Stiles et al., 2018). Both McCabe et al. (2012) and Stiles et al. (2018) found lower percentages of students reporting engaging in plagiarism or cheating in subsequent studies than in 1994. Similarly, Curtis and Tremayne (2021) and Stiles et al. (2018) found lower percentages of students reporting engaging in plagiarism or cheating in 2014 than in 2004.

One notable feature of Figure 1 is that even though the trends appear similar for the three studies, the level of reported plagiarism or cheating differs consistently among the studies. That is, the percentages at any common points in time are highest for Curtis and Tremayne (2021) and lowest for Stiles et al. (2018). There are two possible explanations for these differing levels of reported academic misconduct: 1) differing cohorts of students, where some cheat more frequently as a consequence of national or institutional cultural differences or 2) the different measures elicit more or less admission of misconduct. The latter is more likely.

The surveys used by Stiles et al. (2018) rely on students knowing that they have cheated or plagiarized and then reporting this behavior. However, plagiarism can be inadvertent (Mulholland, 2020). In contrast, the surveys used by McCabe et al. (2012) and Curtis and Tremayne (2021) mostly require students to recognize a behavior they may have engaged in during an assessment, rather than label that behavior as plagiarism or cheating. People may be more likely to admit to socially undesirable behaviors if they do not label them as deviant (MacDonald and Nail, 2005). In addition, the survey used by Curtis and Tremayne (2021) asks students whether they have *ever* engaged in behaviors that are arguably less serious, and thus likely more common, than the behaviors examined in the other two time-lag studies. In contrast, McCabe et al.'s (2012) surveys asked students to report behavior of only the past year. Therefore, it makes sense that Curtis and Tremayne (2021) report the highest prevalence of plagiarism/cheating. Furthermore, the survey used by McCabe et al. (2012) asks about nine different behaviors as compared with only three or four in the surveys used by Stiles et al. (2018). Having more behaviors, any of which would constitute a single instance of plagiarism cheating, means that McCabe et al. (2012) would be more likely to get affirmative responses than Stiles et al. (2018).

Returning to the prevalence trends, an important question to ask is, why might the trend in academic integrity breaches be downward since at least 1994? The authors of the studies themselves offer some differing explanations. Controversially, Stiles et al. (2018) predicted that cheating might be higher among the 2014 sample because the sample is composed of "millennial" students who evince attitudes of "entitlement". Although Stiles et al. (2018) found that students' feelings of entitlement correlated positively with their engagement in cheating and plagiarism, this does not explain why cheating was, in fact, lower in the 2014 study, especially as there was an additional item in the 2014 survey that may have led to more cheating being reported than in their earlier surveys. McCabe et al. (2012) suggest that technological changes, including internet-based plagiarism not covered in their survey, may account for some of the reduced rates of plagiarism and cheating. In addition, McCabe (2016) reports a relationship between institutions having honor codes and lower rates of plagiarism and cheating. Such reports of the impact of honor codes date back to McCabe and colleagues' earlier work, and therefore, some institutions may have implemented honor codes over time in response to previous research. Curtis and Tremayne (2021) attribute the reduction in plagiarism and cheating observed in their study to specific academic integrity education modules taught at Western Sydney University, the increased use of text-matching software, and improved assessment practices.

As the contention that millennials are more entitled, and therefore cheat more, is not borne out in Stiles et al.'s (2018) study, two likely explanations remain for why plagiarism and cheating appear to have trended downward. First, it is possible that the forms of plagiarism and cheating examined in measures created between 15 and 60 years ago are less common, and have been replaced by newer forms of cheating and plagiarism. Second, it is possible that as staff and institutional awareness of academic integrity issues has grown over time, various interventions such as citation training, text-matching software, and honor codes may have had an impact in reducing the prevalence of plagiarism and cheating. The next two sections of this chapter will assess these possibilities as I review data on the prevalence of a newer form of academic misconduct, commercial contract cheating, and then examine the impact of interventions targeted at reducing academic misconduct.

TRENDS IN THE PREVALENCE OF SELF-REPORTED COMMERCIAL CONTRACT CHEATING

As McCabe et al. (2012) note, internet access became more widespread over the past 30 years. In 2007/2008, they added additional questions about internet use to their surveys and found that nearly 95 percent of students who had engaged in cut-and-paste plagiarism had done so from internet sources. It has been argued that just as the internet may facilitate copying and pasting, the internet also has a role in deterring and detecting this behavior with the advent of text-matching software (Curtis and Vardanega, 2016; Park, 2003). McCabe et al. (2012) argued that "If students know that faculty will be checking . . . such cut-and-paste plagiarism may decline" (p. 71). However, a form of cheating that is potentially undetectable by text-matching software is outsourced, ghost-written work.

Various studies throughout the past 30 years have, at least in part, examined students' use of outsourcing behaviors in assessment, such as getting help from family and friends, accessing essay mills, or paying other people to complete homework, term papers, or exams for them. In 2006, Clarke and Lancaster coined the term contract cheating to describe the situation where students enter into a contractual agreement with another party to complete an assignment for the student (for more on Contract Cheating, see Lancaster's chapter in this book). The definition of what constitutes contract cheating has since varied, with Bretag et al. (2019) classifying all outsourcing, whether paid or unpaid, as contract cheating, while specifically paid contract cheating has been more recently referred to as commercial contract cheating (e.g. Lancaster, 2020)

Charting trends in contract cheating in the past 30 years is complicated by the fact that only one of the three studies reviewed in the previous section included a measure of commercial contract cheating. The studies reported by Curtis and Tremayne (2021) found percentages of commercial contract cheating of 3.1 percent (2004), 3.4 percent (2009), 2.8 percent (2014), and 2.8–3.5 percent (2019). These percentages did not differ significantly over time or between any two pairs of years.

Newton (2018), however, conducted a review and meta-analysis of the self-reported prevalence of commercial contract cheating, principally consisting of studies that surveyed students at one point in time. Newton examined 71 studies conducted between 1978 and 2016 and concluded that just over 3.5 percent of students engaged in commercial contract cheating. An identical figure of 3.5 percent was found in an earlier small-scale meta-analysis by Curtis and Clare (2017). Importantly, Newton (2018) reported the prevalence of commercial contract cheating engagement increasing, as indicated by a positive correlation between engagement in cheating and the year in which studies were conducted. However, as discussed previously, estimating trends from studies using different methods, measures, and samples should be done with caution because methodological differences may influence the studies' results. In addition, several large studies have been published since Newton's (2018) review, which provide additional information on the rates of, and possible trends in, commercial contract cheating.

For this chapter, I have updated and re-analyzed Newton's (2018) data to consider more recent studies. Specifically, I obtained Newton's (2018) table of the studies he analyzed, and their details, and added to these the details of the following studies: Foltýnek and Králíková (2018), Bretag et al. (2019), Rundle et al. (2019), Curtis and Tremayne (2021), and Awdry (2020). These five additional studies surveyed over 25,000 students, and increase the total sample reported by Newton (2018) by over 45 percent. After adding these studies' data, I then: 1. reran the analysis of commercial contract cheating prevalence and trends; 2. analyzed the data including only studies 1990–2020; and 3. analyzed the 1990–2020 studies that came from majority English-speaking countries. To explain the third of these analyses, all studies analyzed by Newton (2018) from 1990–2008 were from majority English-speaking countries; however, half of the studies since 2009 were not. In addition, some of the highest percentages of commercial contract cheating were reported in recent studies from non-English-speaking countries, suggesting that these outlier results may be attributable to the peculiarities of the sample, methods, or academic culture. Limiting analyses to the most frequent language group of the nations among the studies allows for closer to like-with-like comparisons.

Table 3 shows the analysis of the prevalence of commercial contract cheating, including: 1. Newton's (2018) findings; 2. revised findings including the subsequent surveys through to 2020; 3. studies limited to 1990–2020; and 4. studies limited to English-speaking countries from 1990–2020. Importantly, in considering trends, the most relevant statistic is the correlation between the year in which the surveys were collected and the percentage of commercial contract cheating reported in the surveys. A positive correlation indicates that as the year of data collection becomes more recent the prevalence of contract cheating becomes higher. Thus, the significant positive correlation, as found by Newton (2018), suggests a trend of increasing student engagement in commercial contract cheating over time. However, Table 3 indicates that the correlation between year and contract cheating percentage was not significant for the period 1990–2020. Moreover, the correlation between year and contract cheating percentage was non-significant and weakly negative when only 1990–2020 studies from English-speaking countries are considered.

This updated analysis of commercial contract cheating prevalence does not suggest an upward trend between 1990–2020. In addition, the analysis indicates that the rate of engagement in this behavior is persistently low—in the range of 2.5–3.5 percent of students self-reporting engaging in commercial contract cheating. A caveat, of course, is, as mentioned earlier, people tend to under-report socially-undesirable behaviors. Still, there are two questions to consider: 1) if cut-and-paste plagiarism is trending down because of text-matching software, why is it not being replaced by commercial contract cheating and 2) given the availability of commercial contract cheating services, why do relatively few students report engaging in this behavior?

Table 3 Trends in commercial contract cheating 1990–2020

	Number of studies	Number of students	Students contract cheating	% contract cheating	Spearman's correlation year-% cheating	p
Newton (2018)	71	54514	1919	3.52	0.368	.0016*
Newton (2018) plus studies 2016–2020	76	79745	2737	3.43	0.303	.008*
Studies 1990–2020	71	78354	2712	3.46	0.206	.085
Studies 1990–2020 —English-speaking countries	54	65843	1620	2.46	−0.135	.332

Note: ★ = significant $p < .05$

Rundle et al. (2019, 2020) offer several answers to the questions above. First, regarding the possibility that commercial contract cheating has not replaced cut-and-paste plagiarism, they suggest that this outcome is consistent with research on "crime displacement". Specifically, when crimes of a certain type, or in a certain place, are reduced, they are not replaced to the same extent by different crimes or by the same crimes occurring elsewhere (Cornish and Clarke, 1987). If this pattern of behavior occurs for academic misconduct, reducing one kind of behavior should not necessarily cause others to increase. Second, Rundle et al. (2019) found that students indicate that they mostly do not engage in commercial contract cheating because they perceive it as immoral non-normative, and undermining their learning goals. In addition, Rundle et al. (2020) suggest that there are more, and stronger, practical and psychological barriers preventing contract cheating than other forms of unethical assessment behavior.

The extended analysis of Newton's (2018) results suggests that commercial contract cheating did not appear to trend upwards as a substitute for the other forms of cheating and plagiarism that trended downwards. Therefore, it is worth examining whether academic integrity interventions that have been implemented in the past 30 years may provide a better explanation for the downward trend in the prevalence of cheating and plagiarism.

STUDIES OF INTERVENTION-RELATED CHANGE IN ACADEMIC MISCONDUCT

Numerous studies in the past 30 years have examined interventions designed to prevent or detect plagiarism and cheating. Importantly, there is substantial evidence that academic integrity interventions have proliferated over this time. For example, the text-matching software Turnitin™ went from 1 million submissions in 2002 to 500 million in 2014 (Turnitin .com, 2020). Stoesz and Yudintseva (2018) identified 21 studies of educational interventions (workshops and tutorials) designed to improve academic integrity reported in published literature between 1995 and 2016, and many of these describe sustained or ongoing interventions created in the last 30 years.

Rather than duplicate existing analyses, two excellent recent reviews of the literature on the effectiveness of academic integrity interventions capture most of the intervention studies in academic integrity literature in the past 30 years. In addition to Stoesz and Yudintseva's (2018) systematic review, mentioned above, Marusic et al. (2016) used the Cochrane methodology to assess interventions designed to promote research and publication integrity, which included many studies focused on reducing plagiarism. Additionally, three papers not cited in these reviews are particularly noteworthy, as they report studies that tracked academic integrity interventions over extended periods (Levine and Pazdernik, 2018; Owens and White, 2013; Perkins et al., 2020).

Academic integrity interventions in the past 30 years seem to come in one of four principal forms: 1) the implementation of honor codes designed to crystalize a shared understanding of acceptable behavior and influence students' attitudes regarding plagiarism and cheating, 2) educational modules (classes, tutorials, online activities) designed to educate students about academic integrity and/or appropriate citation practices, 3) the use of text-matching software, often accompanied by education to help students understand text-matching reports and interpret differences between matched text and plagiarism, and 4) some combination of the above.

Although there has been strong advocacy for the use of honor codes to improve academic integrity, the evidence for their impact is often of limited quality. Studies reported by McCabe et al. (2002), for example, typically show a correlation between the use of honor codes and the prevalence of self-reported plagiarism and cheating. However, any apparent impact of honor codes on rates of cheating may be a problem of self-selection bias rather than an effect of the codes themselves (McCabe, 2016). In other words, institutions with honor codes may attract non-cheating students or encourage under-reporting of cheating by students. Still, there is some longitudinal evidence (i.e. with pre-test and post-test measures) that indicates that implementing honor codes makes students view cheating more negatively (e.g. Raman and Ramlogan, 2020). In addition, honor codes set expectations about standards of acceptable behavior, and studies indicate that academic integrity standards influence students' misconduct behavior (e.g. Curtis et al., 2018). However, asking students to pledge to be honest before submitting assignments may not be enough to reduce misconduct. Evidence that simply making an ethical pledge before submitting work reduces cheating (Shu et al., 2012) has recently been found to have been based on fabricated data (Baskin, 2021). The best evidence for honor codes reducing cheating seems to be when students are regularly reminded about the codes (Tatum and Schwartz, 2017).

The evidence from reviews by Marusic et al. (2016) and Stoesz and Yudintseva (2018) indicates that training in citation skills and paraphrasing are generally helpful, albeit that the effects are modest. Marusic et al. (2016), in particular, concluded that training involving practical exercises and text-matching software showed the most promise in reducing plagiarism (e.g. Barrett and Malcolm, 2006; Batane, 2010; Rolfe, 2011). Stoesz and Yudintseva (2018) concur that educational interventions, which may be automated and delivered online (e.g. Belter and Pré, 2009; Curtis et al. 2013) may be enhanced with hands-on, in-class experiences. These reviews suggest that anti-cheating educational interventions may improve students' attitudes toward integrity, not just their skills, thus having a similar effect to honor codes. However, the reviews generally conclude that skills-based, rather than attitude-based, interventions are more efficacious in reducing cheating and plagiarism.

As noted earlier, in addition to the reviews of academic integrity interventions, three studies have tracked academic integrity interventions over extended periods. These studies overlap in time over the period 2007–2019: 2007–2011 (Owens and While, 2013); 2010–2015 (Levine and Pazdernik, 2018); 2014–2019 (Perkins et al., 2020). In two of these studies, a variety of methods to improve academic integrity, including text-matching software, structured educational modules, mastery tasks, and policy changes were used (Levine and Pazdernik, 2018; Owens and White, 2013). The third study focused solely on the impact of an academic English course (Perkins et al., 2020). All three studies examined cases of academic misconduct as their outcome, and all three studies found a significant reduction in cases over their five-year durations. These studies reinforce the conclusions of the reviews by Marusic et al. (2016) and Stoesz and Yudintseva (2018) that skills-based interventions, accompanied by text-matching software, appear to be effective in reducing academic misconduct.

In summary, it appears that the evidence for skills-based interventions and text-matching software is more substantial and provides clearer demonstrations of impact than the implementation of honor codes. This conclusion accords with some important evidence that students often plagiarize because they do not know how *not* to plagiarize (Delvin and Gray, 2007). Moreover, only assuming academic integrity reflects honor, character, and morality fails to account for the fact that plagiarism can be inadvertent (Barnhardt, 2016; Mulholland, 2020). Taken together, it could be argued that students do not develop character, in the context of academic integrity, just by being told to be of good character; they must be taught *how* to be of good character. This is not to say that higher education should abandon honor codes as the evidence for their effectiveness in reducing cheating, especially when honor codes are regularly made salient, is persuasive (Tatum and Schwartz, 2017). However, it is, at least, important to accompany honor codes with the education students need in the practical skills of academic writing to allow them to meet the terms of these codes.

CONCLUSIONS ON TRENDS IN THE PREVALENCE OF PLAGIARISM AND CHEATING: 1990–2020

In this chapter, I have reviewed the best available evidence of trends in the prevalence of plagiarism and cheating over the 30 years from 1990–2020. Specifically, I aggregated and compared the results of three time-lag studies of plagiarism and cheating, where each study surveyed similar student groups with similar questions, allowing for like-with-like comparisons. These studies indicated that students' engagement in plagiarism and cheating has trended downward since at least 1994. Two main explanations were considered for the downward trend in cheating and plagiarism: 1) whether students are switching to commercial contract cheating to avoid "detectable" forms of plagiarism with the rise of text-matching software and 2) whether interventions designed to reduce plagiarism and cheating are effective and, if so, what types?

On reviewing the best available like-with-like evidence, there was no indication of a clear trend in the prevalence of students' engagement in commercial contract cheating in the last 30 years. This result is consistent both with crime displacement theory and findings that people are less likely to break moral rules that they consider to be more serious (Ariely, 2012). However, there is considerable evidence that educational interventions, combined with text-matching software, were effective in reducing plagiarism and cheating. In addition, there was less clear evidence that honor codes may also be beneficial in lowering plagiarism and cheating. In sum, these results suggest that the work higher education institutions and staff have been doing to try to reduce plagiarism and cheating has had a positive effect. The general finding that educational interventions work to reduce academic misconduct accords with arguments that, in an educational setting, education is preferable to punishment to elicit future academic integrity behaviors of students (Bertram Gallant and Stephens, 2020).

It is important to point out that despite the downward trend in plagiarism and cheating, only one data-point in Figure 1, Stiles et al.'s (2018) 2014 survey, shows less than 50 percent of students engaging in some form of academic misconduct. For all of the other time-lag studies, most students engaged in some form of plagiarism or cheating at least once. Therefore, the finding that plagiarism and cheating is trending downward should not make higher education providers complacent. Every year, new students start their learning journey in colleges and universities, and every year these new students must be trained to understand and apply the expected standards of integrity in their work. In addition, it is worth considering emerging threats to academic integrity that may stop or reverse the downward trend.

CURRENT AND FUTURE THREATS TO ACADEMIC INTEGRITY

One recent development that may contribute to the future recorded trends in the prevalence of academic integrity breaches is the Covid-19 pandemic, which seriously disrupted usual higher education assessment and teaching practices. There are four main reasons to believe that the Covid-19 pandemic may result in an increase in the prevalence of plagiarism and cheating for some years to follow. First, many higher education institutions made a rapid move away from in-person proctored exams to various alternatives, such as unproctored take-home exams and online exams. Clearly, proctored exams significantly reduce students' opportunities to cheat; indeed, evidence suggests that students achieve marks 10–20 percent better in unproctored online exams, and some of this improvement may be attributable to cheating (Daffin and Jones, 2018). Second, it is reasonable to think that a rapid switch to online teaching will not have been executed with a high degree of skill or planning in all instances. Students are likely to find poorly-delivered online courses dissatisfying, and dissatisfaction with the learning and teaching environment predicts engagement in cheating (Anderman and Won, 2019; Bretag et al., 2019). Third, the Covid-19 pandemic is likely to have caused many students significant emotional stress, including fear for their health and the health of their loved ones, social isolation, and potential bereavement. Negative emotions, such as anxiety, increase unethical behavior per se (Kouchaki and Desai, 2015). More specifically, Tindall and Curtis (2020) reported that negative emotional experiences were related to more positive student attitudes toward plagiarism, and Birks et al. (2020) note that mental health concerns are often reported as a factor by students who have engaged in academic misconduct. Moreover, Eaton and Turner (2020) argue that steps taken to address academic integrity during the Covid-19 pandemic, such as e-proctoring, have unknown impacts on students' mental well-being. Finally, essay mills and other contract cheating services have directed advertising at students focused on "helping" students to overcome study problems attributable to the pandemic (McKie, 2020). Indeed, research emerging in 2020–2021 suggests that the prevalence of academic misconduct increased during the Covid-19 pandemic (e.g. Lancaster and Cotarlan, 2021).

There are several reasons to think that some of the factors associated with the Covid-19 pandemic that may increase academic misconduct prevalence will persist. Optimistic estimates initially predicted an end to the Covid-19 pandemic in late 2021, but the emergence of variants of the virus and the need for worldwide vaccination suggests that it will persist as a public health threat for much longer than initially hoped (Charumilind et al., 2020). Numerous commentators have speculated that some substitution of face-to-face with online delivery, and proctored with unproctored assessments, will persist for years beyond the pandemic and may become "the new normal" (e.g. Champagne and Granja, 2021; McMurtrie, 2021). It is, therefore possible that students may develop new habits of cheating and collusion on unproctored tests that will solidify as new norms of behavior that are subsequently conveyed to other students.

Another driver of future trends in the prevalence of plagiarism and cheating is the ongoing technological tug-of-war between those seeking to engage in academic misconduct, or allow others to engage in academic misconduct, and those seeking to deter and detect academic misconduct. Curtis and

Vardanega (2016) suggested that advances in technology that allow students to cheat and plagiarize are potentially matched by technologies that allow cheating to be detected in a process analogous to a co-evolutionary arms race (Vermeij, 1992). The launch of Turnitin™ in 2000 and the gradual uptake of systems for automated text-matching align historically with the downward trend in plagiarism over the past 30 years. However, an important question is, what technological changes will the future hold?

One possible battleground in the next arms race between technologies that facilitate cheating and technologies that may deter or detect cheating is artificial intelligence and machine learning. It has been reported that artificial intelligence can be used to create "passable" academic writing automatically (e.g. Abd-Elaal et al., 2019). Automatic paraphrasing tools can potentially revise unoriginal work sufficiently to evade detection by text-matching software (Rogerson and McCarthy, 2017). Artificial intelligence may also be used by contract cheating providers to find potential "customers" among students based, for example, on their social media posts (Amigud, 2020). By the same token, artificial intelligence and machine learning may be used to detect plagiarism, outsourcing, and machine-written work and to verify students' identity in online learning environments (Amigud et al., 2017). Additionally, artificial intelligence can be used to automate searches for files students inappropriately share online and have these taken down where necessary (Redden, 2021). Whether such an arms race results in a change in the prevalence of student plagiarism and cheating will depend on how fast and effectively cheating and anti-cheating forces manage to bamboozle each other and respond in kind.

CONCLUSION

This chapter has demonstrated a downward trend in the prevalence of higher education students' self-reported plagiarism and cheating behavior in the 30 years 1990–2020. This downward trend is not attributable to a switch to commercial contract cheating, which appears to have remained at a steady, low prevalence in the past 30 years. However, there is evidence to suggest that text-matching software, academic integrity and writing education, and honor codes may have contributed to the downward trend. Nonetheless, higher education teachers and administrators cannot afford to become complacent. The achievements of the past 30 years may not be permanent without continuing efforts to promote academic integrity and deal with emerging threats.

Funding Details

No funding was received to support this research.

Disclosure Statement

The author does not have any conflicts of interest associated with this chapter.

REFERENCES

Abd-Elaal, E. S., Gamage, S. H. and Mills, J. E. (2019). 'Artificial intelligence is a tool for cheating academic integrity'. In *30th Annual Conference for the Australasian Association for Engineering Education (AAEE 2019): Educators Becoming Agents of Change: Innovate, Integrate, Motivate* (p. 397). Engineers Australia.

Abukari, Z. (2016). *Awareness and incidence of plagiarism among students of higher education: A case study of Narh-Bita College.* (Doctoral dissertation, University of Ghana). **http://ugspace.ug.edu.gh/ handle/123456789/21270**

Amigud, A. (2020). 'Cheaters on Twitter: an analysis of engagement approaches of contract cheating services', *Studies in Higher Education, 45*(3), pp. 692–705.

Amigud, A., Arnedo-Moreno, J., Daradoumis, T., and Guerrero-Roldan, A. E. (2017). 'A robust and non-invasive strategy for preserving academic integrity in an open and distance learning environment'. *In 2017 IEEE 17th International Conference on Advanced Learning Technologies* (ICALT) (pp. 530–532). IEEE. Available at: **https://doi. org/10.1109/ICALT.2017.23** (Accessed November 11, 2021).

Anderman, E. M. and Won, S. (2019). 'Academic cheating in disliked classes', *Ethics & Behavior, 29*(1), pp. 1–22.

Ariely, D. (2012). *The (honest) truth about dishonesty.* Harper Collins.

Awdry, R. (2020). 'Assignment outsourcing: Moving beyond contract cheating', *Assessment & Evaluation in Higher Education,* pp. 1–16.

Barnhardt, B. (2016). 'The "epidemic" of cheating depends on its definition: A critique of inferring the moral quality of "cheating in any form"', *Ethics & Behavior, 26*(4), pp. 330–343.

Barrett, R. and Malcolm, J. (2006). 'Embedding plagiarism education in the assessment process', *International Journal for Educational Integrity, 2*(1), pp. 38–45.

Baskin, P. (2021). 'Famed Duke expert on human dishonesty suspected of fraud', *Times Higher Education,* 23 August. Available at: **https://www.timeshighereducation.com/news/famed-duke-expert-human-dishonesty-suspected-fraud** (Accessed Novemner 11, 2021).

Batane, T. (2010). 'Turning to Turnitin™ to fight plagiarism among university students', *Journal of Educational Technology & Society, 13*(2), pp. 1–12.

Belter, R. W. and du Pré, A. (2009). 'A strategy to reduce plagiarism in an undergraduate course', *Teaching of Psychology, 36*(4), pp. 257–261.

Bertram Gallant, T. and M. Stephens, J. (2020). 'Punishment is not enough: The moral imperative of responding to cheating with a developmental approach', *Journal of College and Character, 21*(2), pp. 57–66.

Birks, M., Mills, J., Allen, S. and Tee, S. (2020). 'Managing the mutations: Academic misconduct Australia, New Zealand, and the UK', *International Journal for Educational Integrity, 16*, p. 6.

Bowers, W. J. (1964). *Student dishonesty and its control in college.* Bureau of Applied Social Research, Columbia University.

Bretag, T. (2019). 'Contract cheating will erode trust in science', *Nature*, 574(7780), pp. 599–600.

Bretag, T., Harper, R., Burton, M., Ellis, C., Newton, P., Rozenberg, P., Saddiqui, S. and van Haeringen, K. (2019). 'Contract cheating: A survey of Australian university students', *Studies in Higher Education, 44*(11), pp. 1837–1856.

Champagne, E. and Granja, A. D. (2021). 'How the COVID-19 pandemic may have changed university teaching and testing for good', *The Conversation*, 7 April. Available at: **https://theconversation. com/how-the-covid-19-pandemic-may-have-changed-university-teaching-and-testing-for-good-158342** (Accessed November 11, 2021).

Clarke, R. and Lancaster, T. (2006). 'Eliminating the successor to plagiarism? Identifying the usage of contract cheating sites'. In *proceedings of 2nd international plagiarism conference* (June, pp. 19–21). Northumbria Learning Press.

Charumilind, S., Craven, M., Lamb, J., Sabow A. and Wilson, M. (2020). *When will the COVID-19 pandemic end?* **https:// www.mckinsey.com/industries/healthcare-systems-and-services/our-insights/when-will-the-covid-19-pandemic-end#** (Accessed November 11, 2021).

Cornish, D. B. and Clarke, R. V. (1987). 'Understanding crime displacement: An application of rational choice theory', *Criminology, 25*, pp. 933–948.

Curtis, G. J. and Clare, J. (2017). 'How prevalent is contract cheating and to what extent are students repeat offenders?', *Journal of Academic Ethics*, *15*(2), pp. 115–124.

Curtis, G. J., Cowcher, E., Greene, B. R., Rundle, K., Paull, M. and Davis, M. C. (2018). 'Self-control, injunctive norms, and descriptive norms predict engagement in plagiarism in a theory of planned behavior model', *Journal of Academic Ethics*, *16*(3), pp. 225–239.

Curtis, G. J., Gouldthorp, B., Thomas, E. F., O'Brien, G. M. and Correia, H. M. (2013). 'Online academic-integrity mastery training may improve students' awareness of, and attitudes toward, plagiaris', *Psychology: Learning and Teaching*, *12*(3), pp. 282–289.

Curtis, G. J. and Popal, R. (2011). 'An examination of factors related to plagiarism and a five year follow-up of plagiarism at an Australian university', *International Journal for Educational Integrity*, *7*(1), pp. 30–42.

Curtis, G. J. and Tremayne, K. (2021). Is plagiarism really on the rise? Data from four 5-yearly surveys. *Studies in Higher Education*, *46*(9), pp. 1816–1826.

Curtis, G. J. and Vardanega, L. (2016). Is plagiarism changing over time? A 10-year time-lag study with three points of measurement. *Higher Education Research & Development*, *35*(6), pp. 1167–1179.

Daffin, Jr., L. W. and Jones, A. A. (2018). 'Comparing student performance on proctored and nonproctored exams in online psychology courses', *Online Learning*, *22*(1), pp. 131–145.

Devlin, M. and Gray, K. (2007). 'In their own words: A qualitative study of the reasons Australian university students plagiarize', *Higher Education Research & Development*, *26*(2), pp. 181–198.

Diekhoff, G. M., LaBeff, E. E., Clark, R. E., Williams, L. E., Francis, B. and Haines, V. J. (1996). 'College cheating: Ten years later', *Research in Higher Education*, *37*(4), pp. 487–502.

Eaton, S. E. and Turner, K. L. (2020). 'Exploring academic integrity and mental health during COVID-19: Rapid review', *Journal of Contemporary Education Theory & Research*, *1*, pp. 35–41.

Foltýnek, T. and Králíková, V. (2018). 'Analysis of the contract cheating market in Czechia', *International Journal for Educational Integrity*, *14*(4), pp. 1–15.

Guessoum, N. (2021). How the student cheating epidemic can be tackled. *Arab News, 1 March*. Available at: **https://www.arabnews.com/node/1817976** (Accessed November 11, 2021).

Haines, V., Diekhoff, G. M., LaBeff, E. E. and Clark, R. E. (1986). 'College cheating: Immaturity, lack of commitment, and the neutralizing attitude', *Research in Higher Education, 25*, pp. 342–354.

Hartmann, D. P. (1992). 'Design, measurement, and analysis: Technical issues in developmental research'. In M. H. Bornstein, and M. E. Lamb (Eds), *Development psychology: An advanced textbook* (2nd ed., pp. 59–154). Lawence Erlbaum Associates.

Kouchaki, M. and Desai, S. D. (2015). 'Anxious, threatened, and also unethical: How anxiety makes individuals feel threatened and commit unethical acts', *Journal of Applied Psychology, 100*(2), pp. 360–375.

Lancaster, T. (2020). 'Commercial contract cheating provision through micro-outsourcing web sites', *International Journal for Educational Integrity, 16*, p. 4.

Lancaster, T. and Cotarlan, C. (2021). 'Contract cheating by STEM students through a file sharing website: a Covid-19 pandemic perspective', *International Journal for Educational Integrity, 17*(1), pp. 1–16.

Levine, J. and Pazdernik, V. (2018). 'Evaluation of a four-prong anti-plagiarism program and the incidence of plagiarism: a five-year retrospective study', *Assessment & Evaluation in Higher Education, 43*(7), pp. 1094–1105.

Lim, V. K. and See, S. K. (2001). 'Attitudes toward, and intentions to report, academic cheating among students in Singapore', *Ethics & Behavior, 11*(3), pp. 261–274.

Macale, L., Ghezzi, V., Rocco, G., Fida, R., Vellone, E. and Alvaro, R. (2017). 'Academic dishonesty among Italian nursing students: A longitudinal study', *Nurse Education Today*, *50*, pp. 57–61.

MacDonald, G. and Nail, P. R. (2005). 'Attitude change and the public–private attitude distinction', *British Journal of Social Psychology*, *44*(1), pp. 15–28.

Marusic, A., Wager, E., Utrobicic, A., Rothstein, H. R. and Sambunjak, D. (2016). 'Interventions to prevent misconduct and promote integrity in research and publication', *Cochrane Database of Systematic Reviews*, (4), MR000038.

Matthews, D. (2020). 'Russian politics and Ph.D plagiarism'. *Times Higher Education*, 20 November. Available at: **https://www. insidehighered.com/news/2020/11/20/russian-politics-faces-epidemic-phd-plagiarism** (Accessed November 11, 2021).

Maxwell, A. J., Curtis, G. J. and Vardanega, L. (2006). 'Plagiarism among local and Asian students in Australia', *Guidance & Counselling*, *21*(4), pp. 210–215.

Maxwell, A. J., Curtis, G. J. and Vardanega, L. (2008). 'Does culture influence understanding and perceived seriousness of plagiarism?', *International Journal for Educational Integrity*, *4*(2), pp. 25–40.

McKie, A. (2020) 'Essay mills "targeting students" as pandemic crisis shifts HE online', *Times Higher Education*, 18 June. Available at: **https://www.timeshighereducation.com/news/essay-mills-targeting-students-pandemic-crisis-shifts-he-online** (Accessed November 11, 2021).

McCabe, D. (2016). 'Cheating and honor: Lessons from a long-term research project', (pp. 197–198). In T. Bretag (Ed). *Handbook of Academic Integrity*. SpringerReference.

McCabe, D. L., Butterfield, K. D. and Treviño, L. K. (2012). *Cheating in college: Why students do it and what educators can do about it.* JHU Press.

McCabe, D. L. and Treviño, L. K. (1993). 'Academic dishonesty: Honor codes and other contextual influences', *Journal of Higher Education*, *64*(5), pp. 522–538.

McCabe, D. L and Treviño, L. K. (1997). 'Individual and contextual influences on academic dishonesty: A multi-campus investigation', *Research in Higher Education*, *38*(3), pp. 379–396.

McCabe, D. L., Treviño, L. K. and Butterfield, K. D. (2001). 'Cheating in academic institutions: A decade of research', *Ethics & Behavior*, *11*(3), pp. 219–232.

McCabe, D. L., Treviño, L. K. and Butterfield, K. D. (2002). 'Honor codes and other contextual influences on academic integrity: A replication and extension to modified honor code settings', *Research in Higher Education*, *43*(3), pp. 357–378.

McMurtrie, B. (2021). 'Teaching: After the pandemic, what innovations are worth keeping?,' *Chronicle of Higher Education*, 1 April. Available at: **https://www.chronicle.com/newsletter/teaching/2021-04-01** (Accessed November 11, 2021).

Molnar, K. K. (2015). 'Students' perceptions of academic dishonesty: A nine-year study from 2005 to 2013', *Journal of Academic Ethics*, *13*(2), pp. 135–150.

Mulholland, M. L. (2020). 'Honor and shame: Plagiarism and governing student morality', *Journal of College and Character*, *21*(2), pp. 104–115.

Newton, P. M. (2018). 'How common is commercial contract cheating in higher education and is it increasing? A systematic review, *Frontiers in Education 3*(67).

Owens, C. and White, F. A. (2013). 'A 5-year systematic strategy to reduce plagiarism among first-year psychology university students', *Australian Journal of Psychology*, *65*(1), pp. 14–21.

Park, C. (2003). 'In other (people's) words: Plagiarism by university students-literature and lessons', *Assessment & Evaluation in Higher Education*, *28*(5), pp. 471–488.

REFERENCES

Perkins, M., Gezgin, U. B. and Roe, J. (2020). 'Reducing plagiarism through academic misconduct education', *International Journal for Educational Integrity*, *16*, p. 3.

Raman, V. and Ramlogan, S. (2020). 'Academic integrity and the implementation of the honour code in the clinical training of undergraduate dental students', *International Journal for Educational Integrity*, *16*, p. 9.

Redden, E. (2021). 'Course Hero, meet Course Villain', *Inside Higher Education*, 2 April. Available at: **https://www.insidehighered.com/news/2021/04/02/search-engine-targets-sharing-course-documents-course-hero** (Accessed November 11, 2021).

Rogerson, A. M. and McCarthy, G. (2017). 'Using Internet based paraphrasing tools: Original work, patchwriting or facilitated plagiarism?', *International Journal for Educational Integrity*, *13*, p. 2.

Roig, M. and Caso, M. (2005). 'Lying and cheating: Fraudulent excuse making, cheating, and plagiarism', *The Journal of Psychology*, *139*(6), pp. 485–494.

Rolfe, V. (2011). 'Can Turnitin™ be used to provide instant formative feedback?', *British Journal of Educational Technology*, *42*(4), pp. 701–710.

Roth, R. (2017). *The effect of enrollment status on plagiarism among traditional and non-traditional students*. [doctoral dissertation, Liberty University] Available at: **http://digitalcommons.liberty.edu/doctoral/1407** (Accessed November 11, 2021).

Rundle, K., Curtis G. J. and Clare, J. (2019). 'Why students do not engage in contract cheating', *Frontiers in Psychology*, *10*, p. 2229.

Rundle, K., Curtis, G. J. and Clare, J. (2020). 'Why students choose not to cheat'. In T. Bretag (Ed.). *A research agenda for academic integrity* (pp. 100–111).

Shu, L. L., Mazar, N., Gino, F., Ariely, D. and Bazerman, M. H. (2012). 'Signing at the beginning makes ethics salient and decreases dishonest self-reports in comparison to signing at the end', *Proceedings of the National Academy of Sciences, 109*(38), pp. 15197–15200. **https://doi.org/10.1073/pnas.1209746109**

Stiles, B. L., Wong, N. C. W. and LaBeff, E. E. (2018). 'College cheating thirty years later: The role of academic entitlement', *Deviant Behavior, 39*(7), pp. 823–834.

Stoesz, B. M. and Yudintseva, A. (2018). 'Effectiveness of tutorials for promoting educational integrity: A synthesis paper', *International Journal for Educational Integrity, 14*, p. 6.

Tatum, H. and Schwartz, B. M. (2017). 'Honor codes: Evidence based strategies for improving academic integrity', *Theory Into Practice, 56*(2), pp. 129–135.

Tindall, I. K. and Curtis, G. J. (2020). 'Negative emotionality predicts attitudes toward plagiarism', *Journal of Academic Ethics, 18*(1), pp. 89–102.

Turnitin.com (2020). Available at: **https://www.turnitin.com/ about**. (Accessed 15 December, 2020).

Vandehey, M., Diekhoff, G. and LaBeff, E. (2007). 'College cheating: A twenty-year follow-up and the addition of an honor code', *Journal of College Student Development, 48*(4), pp. 468–480.

Vermeij, G. J. (1992). *Evolution and escalation: An ecological history of life.* Princeton University Press.

Walker, J. (1998). 'Student plagiarism in universities: What are we doing about it?', *Higher Education Research and Development, 17*(1), pp. 89–106.

Walker, M. and Townley, C. (2012). 'Contract cheating: A new challenge for academic honesty?', *Journal of Academic Ethics, 10*(1), pp. 27–44.

Whitley, B. E. (1998). 'Factors associated with cheating among college students: A review', *Research in Higher Education, 39*(3), pp. 235–274.

CHAPTER 3

The Past and Future
of Contract Cheating

Thomas Lancaster

Imperial College London, United Kingdom

http://www.thomaslancaster.co.uk
thomas@thomaslancaster.co.uk

BACKGROUND

Contract cheating represents a major threat to educational standards. It is a phenomenon of which everyone involved with the academic integrity movement needs to be aware, including student affairs professionals, faculty, governing bodies, researchers and students themselves. If left unaddressed, contract cheating threatens to lead to an educational system that within 30 years will be stripped of all its value. All members of the academic community, including students themselves, have a vital role to play to ensure that no student receives an award they do not deserve or develop morally questionable principles to take into professional employment.

The term contract cheating dates to a 2006 research paper (Clarke and Lancaster, 2006). That paper appeared long after the launch of the International Center for Academic Integrity (ICAI) in 1992. There is evidence that academic integrity breaches of a similar form to contract cheating existed before 1992. One of the earliest academic sources discussing the market in essays states that services marketing writing services to students were advertising in New York City newspapers in the 1940s and 1950s (Staviksy, 1973). Contract cheating has developed into a vast international industry, accessible to students and showing massive growth during the Covid-19 pandemic, with written-to-order solutions even being sold to students within the limited timeframe of an examination (Lancaster and Cotarlan, 2021).

Although a single consistent definition of contract cheating does not exist, for the purpose of this chapter, the term is largely considered to address the issue where students are using third parties to complete their educational studies for them, essentially removing themselves from the courses in which they are meant to be assessed. Often this involves a student paying a third party to complete a written assessment or capstone project, but contract cheating can also take place when no payment is involved, or when a student replaces themselves for other forms of assessments, such as examinations.

This chapter is intended to serve as an overview about what is happening with contract cheating now, but also to attempt to forewarn and foreshadow future developments. Although no one can predict the future, the dawn of a machine learning age looks likely to introduce changes to how the contract cheating industry will operate. These changes will become apparent over the next 30 years. Educators and those who support the teaching and learning environment need to be ready to address such changes through improved policies, processes and educational support and by working in partnership with students.

As a discussion-based chapter, this takes the following form. First, the state of contract cheating research is introduced. Second, three technological developments which instructors and staff should be aware of are presented. Finally, the chapter concludes with recommendations to help improve future educational policy and practice.

CONTRACT CHEATING RESEARCH
The Contract Cheating Research Field

It is useful to consider how current research into contract cheating informs our understanding of teaching and learning in practice. Although a full understanding of academic research is not necessary for developing policies and understanding how best to support students and instructors, the history of the field for the past 30 years does help to provide some insight as to how the next 30 years will develop. However, some provisos about academic integrity research in general may also be helpful.

The academic integrity research field is one that suffers from inconsistent use of language and sometimes misleading choices of methodologies and interpretations of data (Lancaster, 2021). This is also true when research into contract cheating is considered. Studies often take findings from a small group of students or from a specific country and attempt to say that these can be generalized to be representative of all students from around the world.

This research background first identifies the quantity of contract cheating research published between 2006 and 2020.

The section then considers some of the key findings from the field, finishing with a discussion of the extent of contract cheating.

Contract Cheating Research Quantity

The contract cheating research field is relatively young. Figure 1 shows the number of peer-reviewed academic papers with "contract cheating" in the paper title published between 2006 and 2020, with 50 percent of these published in 2019 and 2020. The numbers were obtained by searching Google Scholar for academic results, then removing duplicate results, blog posts, transcripts of presentations, and other such sources. Terms other than "contract cheating" have sometimes been used within the field, including "essay mills", "ghostwriting" and "academic outsourcing". These terms are not considered in Figure 1.

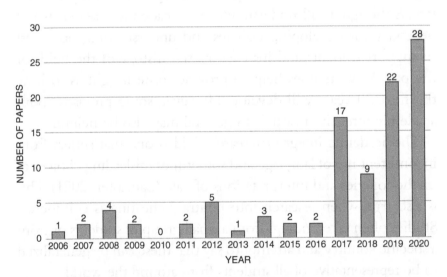

Figure 1 Academic papers with "contract cheating" in the title, by year (2006 to 2020)

Much of the growing interest in contract cheating research can be linked to the MyMaster scandal in Australia, which was first reported in 2014 (McNeilage and Visentin, 2014). Here, the Australian news media were able to access the internal records of a contract cheating provider operating primarily in Sydney, Australia. They obtained details of assignments produced by that service and accessed associated financial records of transactions. The MyMaster service was said to be sophisticated in scale, primarily employing writers from China and advertising to Chinese students taking courses in Australia. Following this incident, higher education providers in Australia were forced to act against contract cheating in a manner that has not yet been seen elsewhere in the world. It remains to be seen if scandals in other countries could have an equally damaging effect or would require institutions to take immediate action.

Contract Cheating Research Results

Since the majority of contract cheating research has been published between 2017 and 2020, this brief overview of the field focuses on that time-period, with relevant publications from 2021 included where they add new knowledge to the field. The developments within this time period also appear to be ones that will foreshadow the next 30 years of activity.

Contract cheating is a large-scale operation. This has been illustrated in multiple research sources, showing that a massive international operation is in place, with firms competing for business. There is no shortage of contract cheating labor or demand for these services. Amigud and Lancaster (2020) showed a widespread market for contract cheating provision operating on Twitter, with a focus on the low-level writing and mathematical assessments common across many disciplines. Lancaster (2020a) identified a surplus of low-cost workers willing to work for contract cheating providers, many operating from Kenya and willing to write a 2,000 word essay for an average price point of $11.46 USD. Rowland et al. (2018) found contract cheating providers exploiting student vulnerabilities to ensure that they would buy from them, providing guarantees, stressing the quality of their offer and avoiding any language that may suggest to students that using these providers was a form of cheating.

Contract cheating is not just a problem for the English speaking world. Students can purchase essays and assignments in many languages and marketing exists with a focus toward students whose first language is not English. Some examples of research moving beyond the English speaking community are illustrative. Comas-Forgas et al. (2020) found search engines running paid adverts for contract cheating providers in Spanish, identifying 60 firms operating from within Spain. Foltýnek and Králíková (2018) observed contract cheating taking place in Czechia. Stella-Maris and Awala-Ale (2017) found cases of contract cheating in Nigeria but said that students justified using such services by noting a poor quality educational experience. Shala et al. (2020) discussed the situation in Kosovo, where students were said to have found contract cheating providers through Facebook and Instagram or, in one case, through their professor.

The contract cheating industry has been shown to operate with little regard toward its customers. One of the biggest challenges has proved to be the possibility of blackmail and extortion, an issue of which Yorke et al. (2020) found few students aware. Khan et al. (2020) have raised awareness of contract cheating as a societal issue, noting how all students suffer if this problem is not addressed. Khan et al. (2020) also discussed how contract cheating can be evidence of students having wider issues in their personal life, so investigations into cheating need to be approached with care and with support available for students rather than purely from a punitive approach. The stress and trauma that students are under was also found by Pitt et al. (2020), but their perspective considered what happens when students are under investigation for contract cheating.

The Extent of Contract Cheating

The exact number of students using contract cheating services is unknown. As the introduction to this section suggested, students have been surveyed to ask them about their use of contract cheating services, but the results always have to be treated with caution. Students may not wish to speak truthfully about such a delicate issue and research by Curtis et al. (2021) has suggested that previous estimates may underlie the true scale of the contract cheating problem.

Many estimates in the literature are based on staff experiences although these should be considered with reference to the fact that contract cheating is not always detected. Harper et al. (2021) found that 52.9 percent of staff had detected contract cheating or assignment outsourcing at least once. Awdry and Newton (2019) found that staff in the United Kingdom and Australia thought that between 5 percent and 10 percent of students were contract cheating although the figures estimated by staff often seem to fall below those reported in surveys by students themselves.

Newton (2018) suggested that the post 2014 figure for students admitting contract cheating was 15.7 percent of all students although this was noted as an international figure so the exact percentages may differ from country to country. Awdry

(2020) found that 12.0 percent of students had got friends and family members to complete assignments for them, an approach that may not involve a commercial transaction but does mean that someone other than the student is completing the work.

Newton (2018) also found that the percentage of students who are contract cheating was increasing by around 0.6 percent every year. This suggests that 37 percent of students could be taking advantage of contract cheating provision by 2050 if current trends continue and the market is left unchecked. If nothing else, this provides an incentive for academic institutions, instructors, and staff to act now.

Research by Curtis et al. (2021) also cast doubt on previous figures by using a survey methodology that encouraged students to tell the truth by entering them into a prize draw. Their estimate was that previous surveys underestimated the extent of contract cheating by a factor of 2.46. In an Australian context, they estimated that 7.9 percent of students were using commercial contract cheating services. When applied to the estimates of Newton (2019), the post 2014 figures could be as high as 38.6 percent.

A further factor that has to be briefly addressed is the impact of Covid-19. Multiple sources, such as Lancaster and Cotarlan (2021) and Hill et al. (2021), have suggested that this has resulted in an increase in contract cheating, with students becoming detached from their academic institution and being heavily marketed to by the contract cheating industry. The number of requests for answers made on a commercial "homework help" website was found to have increased by 196.3 percent during the Covid-19 time period (Lancaster and Cotarlan, 2021), with an immediate increase corresponding with the move to remote teaching and online assessment. Along with the future developments outlined in this chapter, the apparent increase in the use of contract cheating services does suggest the problem needs to be urgently addressed.

FUTURE DEVELOPMENTS
The Need for Future Awareness

Two forces are predicted to shape the future of the contract cheating industry over the next 30 years. The industry will attempt to preserve its revenue streams by addressing the interventions that institutions are putting in place to stop it. Wider advances in artificial intelligence will themselves affect how education is delivered to a generation of students who have been immersed in technology since birth.

Some speculation as to the competencies students will need to succeed in the emerging world is necessary. This may mean that current academic assessment methods are just not suitable for the future. There was a time when calculators were not allowed in an exam hall, but now calculators are accepted and commonplace. At what stage does technology, such as a smart contact lens enabling students to see shop signs translated into their local language, become acceptable in the classroom if such technology could be used openly in wider society? If an employer allows its workers to use such technology to work more efficiently, does this mean that universities should allow it, too? What happens to the students who are not financially privileged enough to avail themselves of such technology?

This section explores three emerging technological developments in more detail which are likely to affect how the contract cheating industry operates and how educational institutions will need to respond.

Automated Writing and Editing Systems

An important component of the contract cheating discussion is going to be developing an understanding of how computers can and should be used in the writing process, where the use of technology should be restricted, and where assurance needs to be had that writing tasks have been completed by a student.

As the rapid development of the contract cheating industry has shown, it is possible to outsource almost any assessed writing task to a third party. The growth of machine learning-based writing solutions means that some tasks do not need to be outsourced at all. Researchers have argued that the current level of automatic writing solutions could be good enough to pass the Turing Test, essentially meaning they can fool other people into thinking they have been written by a human not a computer (Elkins and Chun, 2020).

The technology designed to improve writing is now becoming available in modern word processors and so will be available to students and will be used in industry. A user can access features that will rewrite, edit and improve textual content as they type. Over time, this means that the expression of a rough idea could end up as polished text, removing the need for editing and with very little understanding displayed on the part of the students concerned. Students will need clear guidance about how far such features should be used.

Going beyond editing, it is already possible to use text generation systems, trained on millions of pieces of example text, to produce reports that are almost indistinguishable from those written by humans. One example lies in the field of automated journalism, where routine stories, such as those on sporting results or share price updates, can be crafted by computers.

An example given by Carlson (2014) discusses how such technology was used to enable reporting of an earthquake in the Los Angeles area.

It is of great concern if students misuse automated writing systems such as these. It is of perhaps greater concern if the contract cheating industry itself has access to such technology. They would then have the choice between selling assessments to students that have been produced by humans or by machines. If the technology continues to develop in sophistication over the next 30 years, students and assessors alike may not know the difference.

A dilemma needs to be pondered regarding whether writing should remain an important aspect of education and assessment at all. If machines are commonly used for writing, should human-led writing be considered as a premium skill at university level and assessed as such? Should students be required to demonstrate that they are proficient at generating written texts rather than preparing them from scratch? Or would anything be lost from education if writing quality was no longer assessed at all?

Contract Cheating Detection

Detection is sometimes looked at as a magic bullet solution to the problem of contract cheating. Current approaches to automating contract cheating detection, summarized in Lancaster (2020b), are showing promise. Considering the next 30 years of developments, automated detection of ghost-written work would seem to offer one part of a solution but not a complete one. This is particularly the case when the contract cheating industry is also looking to explore and exploit such technology for themselves.

Several current approaches to detecting contract cheating seem to show promise, but these are not widely used. One example is the use of stylometric techniques to identify the author of a given document, an idea most prominently seen in a tool made available by a commercial provider (Dawson et al., 2020). The idea behind stylometric analysis is that all individuals have a unique writing style. This can be represented by measures derived from a text, perhaps as simple as the average number of words per sentence. Over time, a profile of how a student writes can be developed. If a new written assignment is handed in that differs stylistically from the earlier work, that is an indication that a third party may have written that assignment which can then be checked by a human.

Other detection techniques are also used. These include the forensic investigation of computer files to see if there are indicators of a writer other than the student, as researched for example by Johnson and Davies (2020). More invasive techniques can track the typing patterns of students or monitor where files are accessed from. Students can be automatically sent questions about their writing, which they should be able to answer if familiar with the material. It may also be possible to automatically analyze the reference lists within files to see if these are sensible. There are many opportunities for technical researchers in this field, and access to improved technologies for detection is likely to become available over the next thirty years.

The long-term challenge comes when the contract cheating industry becomes wise to the detection measures being used. It is possible for them to apply their own file manipulations to reduce the usefulness of many interventions. For example, a contract cheating provider could doctor the properties of a file to make it look like only the student had worked on it. Where stylometric analysis is in place, a student could ensure that they always hired the same writer. This would make sure they were always submitting work with the same writing style. Contract cheating providers may also see the value of promoting this so they can encourage students to become repeat customers. Then there is the issue of documents being written and rewritten by machines. How easy will it be for writing style to just be another parameter that is fed into the system?

Detection does always have a valid purpose. If nothing else, the risk of academic misconduct being detected can provide enough of an incentive to stop students from taking the risk of using a contract cheating provider. Other changes may push up the cost of buying work so that students stop and think whether this is in their best interests. But it is not sensible to rely on detection alone, especially as the wider contract cheating landscape itself adapts and changes.

Cybersecurity Risks to Institutions and Students

The issue of cybersecurity has become a real challenge for academic institutions. The institutional staff who are charged with responsibility for cybersecurity need to be aware of contract cheating as many of the systems that are used to record marks and maintain quality are at the risk of being hacked. Students, too, too need to be made aware of the risks to their personal data and the unscrupulous offers that are out there.

Students are taking advanced technological courses at university in areas, such as forensic computing, ethical hacking, and computer security. University computer systems are a natural place against which some students may wish to test out their skills, whether this is done with good or bad intentions.

A university education is not a requirement to become proficient at computer hacking. A risk comes when contract cheating providers are hired to unlawfully access university computer systems. The damage that can be done is great. Providers can access teaching materials, assessments, student work, exams, and model answers. Such material has real value to them when they are looking to improve their offer to customers. Sometimes materials can be even accessed with the inadvertent help of their customers, who provide contract cheating providers with their university log in details so they can submit assessments directly for them.

Low-level hacking is also of concern, for example in the case where a contract cheating firm unlawfully accesses a student record system and changes a failed mark into a passing grade. Those within the institution responsible for ensuring the integrity of transcripts do have to consider how checking processes on awarded marks and qualifications will be enacted.

More widely, students need to be made aware about how suspect the whole contract cheating industry is, especially if they provide personal information to them. If a student ever succumbs to the marketing provided by the contract cheating industry, they will end up handing across information that allows them to be tracked. Even just a course code or an instructor name provides power to the contract cheating industry and puts students at the risk of extortion or blackmail.

RECOMMENDATIONS

This chapter has shown that contract cheating is a current risk to educational institutions and that it will remain a risk over the next 30 years. Universities and colleges need to be ready to act and to address the negative impact that contract cheating stands to have on their character. Contract cheating can only be addressed by considering both internal educational systems and the wider societal and educational landscape that affords students the opportunity to bypass academic integrity. This requires a whole community approach.

Technology changes will always happen. Such changes have an impact on educational provision. It is important for institutions to put proactive measures in place to show they are aware of contract cheating developments but trying to battle against change is not sensible. Therefore, the only rational solution would seem to be to find the best ways to operate with this technology and to ensure that students are taught about academic integrity and supported to ensure they act with integrity.

Instructors and those who support the teaching and learning environment are at the forefront of the work needed here, which needs to be conducted with buy-in from all members of the academy, including other staff, governing bodies, and students themselves. The policies and processes surrounding contract cheating need to be proactively developed and regularly reviewed. Special consideration needs to be made to what should happen if students are suspected of contract cheating, how this will be fairly and accurately addressed, who will support the student during the pressure of a misconduct investigation, what penalties will be awarded, and what interventions will be put into place to ensure that contract cheating does not happen to the student again.

The development of new policies brings with it an excellent opportunity for practice to be shared more widely across the sector. Such practice can include success stories from individual institutions. It would be useful if institutions could compare internal figures showing how far they have managed to address contract cheating with other universities. That would help to provide a level of benchmarking for the sector. Contract cheating is widespread and, if individual institutions show numbers of cases that are low or non-existent, this suggests that the institution may have major process failures. The ostrich method of ignoring possible problems does not help to raise confidence in the sector and does not show respect for all the honest and hard-working students who are out there.

There are already many positive initiatives taking place around the world. The International Day of Action against Contract Cheating, initiated by the International Center for Academic Integrity (ICAI)[1], has taken place annually since 2016. This provides a focal point online and within institutions for discussion about this important issue. A wealth of resources surrounding the event are available on the ICAI website ("Day Against Contract Cheating", n.d.). As part of the event, institutions are encouraged to run their own local events to raise awareness; these events can be organized by staff or students. Many participants share their activities through university web sites and on social media. The 2020 event featured 20 hours of live broadcasts on issues surrounding contract cheating and these are archived to watch online.

Perhaps the best solution to ensuring academic integrity for the next 30 years is to work with the student body in equal partnership. That is something which, it is hoped, the entire educational community can strive for.

---

[1] **https://academicintegrity.org/**

REFERENCES

Amigud, A. and Lancaster, T. (2020). 'I will pay someone to do my assignment: an analysis of market demand for contract cheating services on twitter', *Assessment & Evaluation in Higher Education*, *45*(4), pp. 541–553.

Awdry, R. (2021). 'Assignment outsourcing: moving beyond contract cheating', *Assessment & Evaluation in Higher Education*, 46(2), pp. 220–235.

Awdry, R. and Newton, P. (2019). 'Staff views on commercial contract cheating in higher education: a survey study in Australia and the UK', *Higher Education*, 78(4), pp. 593–610.

Carlson, M. (2015). 'The Robotic Reporter', *Digital Journalism*, *3*(3), pp. 416–431.

Clarke, R. and Lancaster, T. (2006). 'Eliminating the successor to plagiarism? Identifying the usage of contract cheating sites'. In *Proceedings of 2nd International Plagiarism Conference*, pp. 19–21, Northumbria Learning Press.

Comas-Forgas, R., Sureda-Negre, J., and Morey-López, M. (2020). 'Spanish contract cheating website marketing through search engine advertisements', *Assessment & Evaluation in Higher Education*.

Curtis, G., McNeill, M., Slade, C., Tremayne, K., Harper, R., Rundle, K. and Greenaway, R. (2021). 'Moving beyond self-reports to estimate the prevalence of commercial contract cheating: an Australian study', *Studies in Higher Education*, pp. 1–13.

"Day Against Contract Cheating" (n.d.) Retrieved from: **https://academicintegrity.org/events-conferences/idoa-international-day-of-action-against-contract-cheating**

Dawson, P., Sutherland-Smith, W., and Ricksen, M. (2020). 'Can software improve marker accuracy at detecting contract cheating? A pilot study of the Turnitin™ authorship investigate alpha', *Assessment & Evaluation in Higher Education*, *45*(4), pp. 473–482.

Elkins, K. and Chun, J. (2020). 'Can GPT-3 Pass a Writer's Turing Test?', *Journal of Cultural Analytics*, *5*(2).

Foltýnek, T. and Králíková, V. (2018). 'Analysis of the contract cheating market in Czechia', *International Journal for Educational Integrity*, *14*(4).

Harper. R., Bretag, T. and Rundle, K. (2021). 'Detecting contract cheating: examining the role of assessment type', *Higher Education Research & Development*, *40*(2), pp. 263–278.

Hill, G., Mason, J. and Dunn, A. (2021). 'Contract cheating: an increasing challenge for global academic community arising from COVID-19', *Research and Practice in Technology Enhanced Learning*, *16*(1).

Johnson, C. and Davies, R. (2020). 'Using digital forensic techniques to identify contract cheating: A case study', *Journal of Academic Ethics*, *18*(2), pp. 105–113.

Khan, Z., Hemnani, P., Raheja, S., and Joshy, J. (2020). 'Raising Awareness on Contract Cheating–Lessons Learned from Running Campus-Wide Campaigns', *Journal of Academic Ethics*, *18*(1), pp. 17–33.

Lancaster, T. and Cotarlan, C. (2021). 'Contract cheating by STEM students through a file sharing website: a Covid-19 pandemic perspective', *International Journal for Educational Integrity*, *17*(3).

Lancaster, T. (2020a). 'Commercial contract cheating provision through micro-outsourcing web sites', *International Journal for Educational Integrity*, *16*(4).

Lancaster, T. (2020b). *Yes, contract cheating can be detected* [Slides]. Slideshare. Available at: **https://www.slideshare.net/ThomasLancaster/ yes-contract-cheating-can-be-detected-eighth-annual- congress-of-academic-integrity-24-september-2020**.

Lancaster, T. (2021). 'Academic dishonesty or academic integrity? Using Natural Language Processing (nlp) techniques to investigate positive integrity in academic integrity research', *Journal of Academic Ethics*.

REFERENCES

McNeilage, A. and Visentin, A. (2014). 'Students enlist MyMaster website to write essays, assignments', The Sydney Morning Herald, November 12. Retrieved from: **https://www.smh.com.au/ education/students-enlist-mymaster-website-to-write-essays-assignments-20141110-11k0xg.html**

Newton, P. (2018). 'How common is commercial contract cheating in higher education and is it increasing? A systematic review'. In *Frontiers in Education, 3*(67).

Pitt, P., Dullaghan, K., and Sutherland-Smith, W. (2020). '"Mess, stress and trauma": students' experiences of formal contract cheating processes', *Assessment & Evaluation in Higher Education*, pp. 1–14.

Rowland, S., Slade, C., Wong, K. and Whiting, B. (2018). 'Just turn to us': the persuasive features of contract cheating websites', *Assessment & Evaluation in Higher Education, 43*(4), pp. 652–665.

Shala, S., Hyseni-Spahiu, M., and Selimaj, A. (2020). 'Addressing contract cheating in Kosovo and international practices', *International Journal for Educational Integrity, 16*(11).

Stavisky, L. P. (1973). 'Term paper mills, academic plagiarism, and state regulation', *Political Science Quarterly, 88*(3), pp. 445–461.

Stella-Maris, O. and Awala-Ale, A. (2017). 'Exploring students' perception and experience of ghostwriting and contract cheating in Nigeria higher education institutions', *World Journal of Educational Research, 4*(4).

Yorke, J., Sefcik, L., and Veeran-Colton, T. (2020). 'Contract cheating and blackmail: a risky business?', *Studies in Higher Education*.

CHAPTER 4

Academic Motivation and Cheating: A Psychological Perspective

Eric M. Anderman, Shantanu Tilak, Andrew H. Perry, Jacqueline von Spiegel, and Arianna Black

The Ohio State University

INTRODUCTION

A focus on the relationships between academic motivation and cheating behaviors has only become a major research focus over the past 20 years (Krou et al., 2020). Whereas some early studies did examine motivation and cheating (e.g. Fakouri, 1972), studies examining the relations between academic cheating and motivation have benefited from recent theoretical and empirical developments in motivation research (e.g. Wigfield and Koenka, 2020). The study of academic motivation is approached through several theoretical lenses. While some of the differences between these theories are striking, there also are many similarities.

In terms of understanding the relation between cheating and motivation, these theories offer useful approaches because each focuses on distinct aspects of motivation.

In this chapter, we focus on five of the most prominent theories: attribution theory, achievement goal orientation theory, Expectancy-Value Theory, social-cognitive theory, and self-determination theory. We take this approach because academic motivation is not a "one size fits all" discussion. Rather, each theory addresses unique aspects of motivation and offers unique implications for the study of and prevention of academic dishonesty. We focus on postsecondary contexts although we do also refer to some studies conducted in P-12 settings, as that research is relevant in helping college personnel understand why students may be motivated to cheat. We then examine the benefits of incorporating multiple theoretical frameworks into studies of academic integrity and discuss implications for policy and practice.

In each of the following sections, we first describe the major tenets of each theory. We then discuss aspects of academic integrity that each theory can help to explain. We conclude each section by describing some of the research that has been conducted using each framework to examine academic integrity. We acknowledge that these theories are complex, and we do not attempt to provide comprehensive reviews of these theories. Rather, we provide a brief overview of each theory and how each is related to academic integrity.

ATTRIBUTION THEORY

Attribution theorists are interested in understanding students' thinking with regard to the reasons why an event occurred or the reasons why the student decided to engage in a particular behavior (e.g. cheating). The types of attributions that individuals make are predictive of future behaviors (Weiner, 1990). Whereas the overall model of attributions is quite complex and beyond the scope of this chapter (see Graham, 2020, for a review), it is important to note that the theory encompasses both ascriptions of causality and emotional reactions. While most motivation frameworks focus on cognitions that occur prior to engaging in a behavior such as cheating, attribution theory focuses on how the students explain to themselves the reasons why they engaged in the behavior in the first place (after the behavior occurred).

When an event occurs (e.g. a student cheats on a test), attribution theorists argue that the individual attributes the reasons for the event to three causal dimensions (Weiner, 1996). The first dimension is referred to as locus, which can either be internal (e.g. "I cheated because I'm not a moral person") or external (e.g. "I cheated because I have a bad instructor"). The second dimension, referred to as controllability, which can be categorized as either controllable (e.g. "I cheated because I didn't study, even though I could have") or uncontrollable (e.g. "I'm just stupid"). The third dimension, referred to as stability, can be categorized as either stable ("The test was in math, and I have always found math to be difficult") or unstable (e.g. "I had a terrible headache the day before the test and I just couldn't study, so I cheated"). For any event, a student makes an attribution (e.g. "I cheated because I have a bad instructor"). That attribution can subsequently be classified along the three dimensions. In terms of locus, having a bad instructor would be external; and in terms of controllability, having a bad instructor would be perceived as uncontrollable (i.e. a student can't control the quality of the instructor). These causal ascriptions lead to a variety of emotional responses (e.g. feeling depressed), which in turn are predictive of future behaviors (e.g. cheating).

Attributions and Academic Integrity

Attribution theory allows researchers to examine the internal justifications that students have for cheating. Whenever a student cheats, the student justifies that action by having a personal, subjective rationale for why the behavior was justified (e.g. "I cheated because I went out with friends last night instead of studying"). As we review below, most studies of academic integrity and attributions suggest that college students justify their cheating to themselves by ascribing the causes of their decisions to cheat to external circumstances. The tendency to justify engagement in an obviously inappropriate behavior (i.e. cheating) is referred to as a neutralizing attitude.

Students who repeatedly engage in cheating behaviors may develop replicable patterns of attributions to explain those behaviors. If students come to believe that they simply have no math ability, they may be more likely to cheat repeatedly. There has been some research examining such relationships between students' attributions and cheating. Although this research is scant, results suggest that students often attribute cheating to the instructor. Murdock and colleagues (Murdock, Beauchamp and Hinton, 2008) found that when high school students perceived teachers as competent and caring, students were less likely to attribute cheating to the teacher. Evans and Craig (1990a) also found that high-achieving, college-bound adolescents in particular were likely to attribute the decision to cheat to the teacher. In a related study, Murdock et al. (Murdock, Miller and Goetzinger, 2007) found that both undergraduate and graduate students were more likely to attribute blame (for student cheating) to the course instructor when the pedagogy was perceived as being poor.

Other studies have examined attributions and cheating from different perspectives. Evans and Craig (1990b) examined attributions for cheating in high school students. They found that students were more likely than were their teachers to attribute cheating to assessment practices (i.e. how the teacher graded exams and assignments) and heavy academic workloads. Using a sample of Iranian graduate students, Babaii and Nejadghanbar (2017) found that students attributed acts of plagiarism to a number of causes. For example, in addition to poor instruction, students also attributed plagiarism to being unfamiliar with the behaviors that constitute plagiarism as well as to simply having insufficient time to complete work or to being lazy.

In summary, attribution theory provides a window through which we can explore how students justify cheating. Its focus on students' beliefs about the causes of events helps us understand how beliefs about the causes of those events may lead to subsequent academic dishonesty. Research on academic integrity from an attribution theory perspective lends support to the prevalence of neutralizing attitudes among college students who engage in cheating (Stephens, 2017).

ACHIEVEMENT GOAL THEORY

Achievement Goal Theory (AGT) enables scholars to better understand how students' goals for academic tasks may motivate cheating. The initial version of AGT (Kaplan et al., 2002) aligns goals that focus on mastery (i.e. the development of personal ability) and performance (i.e. the demonstration of ability in comparison with others). Later iterations of the theory added approach and avoidance dimensions of two goals (Urdan and

Kaplan, 2020). The four constructs that comprise the theory and that have guided most of the research on academic integrity include:

1. mastery-approach goals, which involve striving for personal knowledge development
2. mastery-avoidance goals, which involve trying to evade losing meaning in one's work
3. performance-approach goals, which involve aiming to outdo others
4. performance-avoidance goals, which involve trying not to be perceived as incompetent by others

According to AGT, each of these four goals drive students' motivation to complete academic tasks (Treasure et al., 2001). These goals are not just part of students' inner perceptions, but also dependent on external factors in the classroom. Instructional practices like a strong emphasis on testing or showing favoritism to higher-scoring students, for example, may affect the goals that students adopt. If an instructor emphasizes testing and talks about tests frequently, then a student in that class might adopt performance-approach or avoidance goals. Even specific tasks may elicit different goal orientations from students (e.g. a student may react differently to a calculus problem than to a social studies essay) (Elliot et al., 2011).

Mastery-approach goals are associated with generally positive outcomes, such as greater engagement and the use of more adaptive cognitive strategies, whereas performance goals may induce a high-stakes environment pressurizing students to utilize maladaptive self-regulatory strategies (see Anderman and Wolters, 2006, for a review). Sometimes students hold both types of goal orientations at once. For example, an instructor may stress the importance of grades yet also provide opportunities for autonomy by allowing students to pursue topics they find interesting. This may lead students to adopt multiple goal orientations simultaneously (e.g. wanting to demonstrate one's ability by getting a good grade on a paper one thinks is interesting) (Harackiewicz and Linnenbrink, 2006; Pintrich, 2000). While there is a body of work examining the effect of performance-approach/avoidance goals and mastery approach goals on learning and classroom behaviors, there has been limited work specifically investigating the unique roles of mastery-avoidance goals.

AGT provides a framework to understand the relationships between certain behaviors (e.g. cheating) and students' goals and intentions (e.g. whether to get a high grade and impress one's peers or parents, or develop one's competence). These relationships can also be characterized by students' perceptions of the goals emphasized by their instructors. These perceptions of the goals stressed in a particular course are referred to as goal structures. When students perceive the instructor as emphasizing the importance of trying hard, learning from one's mistakes, and mastering the content, students perceive a mastery goal structure. In contrast, when students perceive the course instructor as emphasizing grades and differences in students' abilities, students perceive a performance goal structure (Bardach et al., 2020).

Achievement Goal Theory and Academic Integrity

AGT provides a framework to understand cheating through the lens of a student asking "what is my purpose?" in engaging with an academic task (Murdock and Anderman, 2006). In general, studies indicate that academic integrity is related positively to mastery goals, whereas academic misconduct more likely to be related positively to a variety of performance and extrinsic goals. Van Yperen et al. (2011) conducted studies on undergraduate students examining the role of achievement goals in predicting cheating behaviors, finding that higher incidences of cheating behaviors were associated with performance goals. Miller et al. (2011) investigated 1,086 U.S. college students, finding that students who related cheating to punitive consequences rather than learning and personal character were more likely to cheat.

Park (2020) analyzed differences across various majors in a sample of 2,360 Korean students, finding that self-growth or mastery goals were related to lesser cheating, with pre-med students showing lower frequency of serious cheating (e.g. colluding on an exam) than business majors, and engineering students showing a higher degree of minor cheating (e.g. copying an assignment). The adaptive effects of mastery goals may also translate into college athletics. Ring and Kavussanu (2018) conducted several studies on college athletes and found that students with performance goals were more likely to cheat in hypothetical situations. Moreover, those with the desire to best others in actual races tended to misreport their finish times. Daumiller and Janke (2019) suggest that the nature of evaluation by instructors (result-based or process-based) and goal orientations are related to cheating. They found that students adopting performance goals while working on result-based tasks were most likely to display dishonesty. Jordan (2001) found college students' goal orientations differed across various courses, and suggested that students were more likely to engage in dishonest behaviors in classes for which they adopted a performance goal orientation. Moreover, disliking a class may lead students to believe it is acceptable to cheat (Anderman and Won, 2019).

Perceived classroom goal structures also affect students' personal goals, in turn affecting dishonest behavior. Pulfrey et al. (2019) observed that pedagogy offering greater autonomy to students, or promoting a mastery goal structure, reduced the tendency to cheat. However, students adopting individual performance goals were less responsive to such pedagogical techniques. Bong (2008) investigated relations between sociocultural variables (parental relationships), achievement goals (at the classroom and personal levels) and cheating behaviors. Students who perceived classroom performance goal structures exhibited more cheating behaviors mediated and enhanced through individual performance-approach goals.

In summary, when college educators and administrators are cognizant of students' personal goals and perceptions of goal structures, we are better able to understand why some students engage in academic misconduct. When students hold mastery goals or perceive that their instructors emphasize mastery, academic dishonesty is less likely to occur, in comparison to students who hold performance goals or who perceive that their instructors emphasize ability differences and exam scores.

SOCIAL-COGNITIVE THEORY

In social-cognitive theory (SCT), students' academic choices can be explained through the reciprocal interactions of the person, their behavior, and the environment (Bandura, 1986). Through their experiences with their environment and by observing others' experiences, students learn to predict the outcomes of their academic choices. An assumption of SCT is that students will choose to engage in behaviors that they believe will lead to successful outcomes. Self-efficacy, the beliefs in one's own capabilities and their expected outcomes, is a central component of SCT, as it can explain academic choices and behaviors (Bandura, 1986). Students who have high self-efficacy beliefs for a task (e.g. a specific assignment) are more likely to engage with the task because they expect success, whereas students with low self-efficacy beliefs doubt their capabilities and so may avoid engaging with the task. Self-efficacy affects students' self-regulation during learning and flexibility of thinking. Students who are more confident in their abilities tend to work harder and persist through challenges because they expect positive outcomes from their efforts (Usher and Pajares, 2008). Importantly, self-efficacy is subject-specific and task-specific and does not generalize across all aspects of a student's life. Thus, in a biology class, a student may hold high efficacy beliefs taking a unit test on anatomy, but low efficacy beliefs for taking a unit test on cellular biology. Students develop self-efficacy for academic tasks through their own experiences with learning as well as observing others' experiences and outcomes.

Self-efficacy beliefs are often based on students' past experiences with a task or *mastery experiences* (Usher and Pajares, 2008). After completing a task, a student will judge whether the outcome was successful. If the outcome is a success, the student will feel more confident in their abilities to succeed at the task or similar tasks. However, if the student interprets the outcome as failing to achieve the goal, the student may doubt their capabilities and potential for future success. If a task is particularly challenging, a successful outcome can be a powerful mastery experience, having a lasting positive impact on self-efficacy (Bandura, 1997). However, if the student feels the need to put forth a great deal of effort or requires assistance on a task, this informs the student that they have lower capabilities than needed for the task, resulting in lower self-efficacy (Usher and Pajares, 2008).

In addition to learning through personal experiences of interactions with the environment, SCT contends that students learn through observation others' experiences, or *vicarious experiences* (Usher and Pajares, 2008). Students observe the outcomes of other students' behaviors, thereby learning the likely consequences if they engage in the behaviors themselves. When students observe a behavior (e.g. studying) produce a favorable outcome for other students, they are more likely to engage in that behavior themselves. Similarly, if students observe that engaging in prohibited behaviors (e.g. cheating) results in negative consequences, they will be less likely to engage in the same behaviors. However, if these behaviors go unpunished, students are more likely to expect a positive outcome and, thus, are more likely to engage in the prohibited behaviors (Bandura, 1986).

Social-Cognitive Theory and Academic Integrity

As students reflect on their capabilities, they make predictions about the outcomes of their efforts (Bandura, 1997). Students who do not expect to be successful at a task, either due to self-efficacy beliefs or situational factors, are more likely to cheat to obtain a desirable outcome (Murdock and Anderman, 2006). For example, if a student does not feel capable of achieving a passing grade on a term paper, either due to their own capabilities or the instructor's expected grading, the student may plagiarize in order to secure the passing grade.

In research examining the antecedents of cheating, self-efficacy has emerged as an important motivational factor (Lee et al., 2020;

Whitley, 1998). Consistently, academic self-efficacy has been shown to be negatively related to cheating. In a meta-analysis, Lee et al. (2020) found that higher academic self-efficacy was related to less dishonest behavior. Murdock, Hale, and Weber (2001) found that middle school students who reported more cheating behaviors had lower academic self-efficacy. Similarly, Nora and Zhang (2010) found that high school students with lower academic self-efficacy were more likely to cheat than students who felt confident about their capabilities. When examining different forms of cheating (i.e. copying work, plagiarism), self-efficacy negatively predicts each type of behavior underlining the consistent impact self-efficacy has on academic decision-making (Marsden et al., 2005). Additionally, self-efficacy not only predicts cheating behaviors, but also attitudes toward academic dishonesty. In a study on university students' attitudes toward plagiarism, du Rocher (2018) found that higher self-efficacy was related to more negative attitudes toward plagiarism.

While there is a consistent inverse relationship between academic performance and cheating, there are many lower-performing students who do not cheat and higher-achieving students who do (Whitley, 1998). Finn and Frone (2004) examined the relations of academic self-efficacy and performance to cheating, finding that self-efficacy is a protective factor against cheating for higher-performing students, while high-performing students with low self-efficacy were more likely to cheat.

Students' beliefs in their ability to cheat also factor into their decisions. When deciding whether or not to cheat, students recall prior experiences with cheating to determine if it will yield the desired outcome. Ogilvie and Stewart (2010) found that academic self-efficacy was negatively related to plagiarism, and that the only significant predictor of plagiarism in university students with low academic self-efficacy was prior experience with plagiarism. Students with low academic self-efficacy may instead develop a higher self-efficacy for cheating through successful experiences with plagiarism. Nora and Zhang (2010) found that students who observed a peer succeed at cheating (i.e. getting a good grade and escaping punishment) were more likely to cheat, supporting the development of cheating self-efficacy through vicarious learning. In a review of 25 years of studies of cheating, Whitley (1998) found that two of the major predictors of cheating are having cheated in the past (i.e. mastery experiences) and the perception of cheating being a common practice among peers (i.e. vicarious learning).

When students do not feel academically capable, they are more likely to cheat. With successful experiences with cheating, students become emboldened and feel more efficacious in their cheating behaviors, creating a behavior pattern of academic dishonesty (Whitley, 1998). The key to breaking this cycle is the improvement of academic self-efficacy (Anderman and Koenka, 2017; Finn and Frone, 2004). Alt (2015) found that university students who were motivated to regulate and reflect on their learning were more likely to have high academic self-efficacy and were less likely to cheat. In addition, students with high regulatory self-efficacy (i.e. belief in their capability to resist the temptation to misbehave) are less likely to cheat (Farnese et al., 2011; Fida et al., 2018). These findings suggest that the development of metacognitive learning strategies may increase students' confidence in their academic abilities, thereby decreasing their reliance on cheating as a viable option.

In summary, higher self-efficacy beliefs are related to less cheating. When students feel confident about their abilities to learn and to succeed at a specific task (or within a specific course), they are less likely to cheat. Cheating is not necessarily useful or worth the risk when students feel confident. Instructional practices that support the development of positive self-efficacy beliefs have the potential to decrease academic dishonesty.

SITUATED EXPECTANCY-VALUE THEORY

Expectancy-Value Theory recently renamed as Situated Expectancy-Value Theory (SEVT; Eccles and Wigfield, 2020) provides another framework for understanding academic and achievement-related choices. According to SEVT, students' academic choices, effort, persistence, and achievement can be explained by their expectancies for success and their subjective task values (Wigfield and Eccles, 2000). Expectancies for success, akin theoretically to self-efficacy, are the beliefs held about how well one thinks they will perform on a task or in a subject domain (e.g. math). Not unlike self-efficacy, expectancies are both domain and task or situation specific (Eccles and Wigfield, 2020). Expectancies for success have been identified as reliable predictors of performance even when prior achievement is considered although there is a reciprocal and cyclical relationship between expectancies and actual performance (Wigfield and Eccles, 2000).

Subjective task values have been identified as robust predictors of students' choices, intentions to persist, and actual persistence behaviors (Wigfield and Eccles, 2000). Subjective task values have been separated theoretically and empirically into utility value, attainment value, interest/intrinsic value, and costs. An individual who deems that a task has utility value engages with the task due to the perceived usefulness of the task as it pertains to a future goal. Attainment value to task engagement due to the personal importance that the task holds for the individual, such as the task contributing to one's sense of identity. Finally, interest or intrinsic value leads to task engagement due to the enjoyment derived (Wigfield and Eccles, 2000).

Costs, including emotional cost, loss of valued alternatives, and effort cost, are an additional component of task values and suggest the more negative side of task engagement, which can lead to task avoidance (Eccles and Wigfield, 2020). Emotional costs are perceived when someone anticipates that engaging in a task will produce negative psychological ramifications, such as heightened anxiety or the anticipated social costs of failure. Cost in the form of loss of a valued alternative denotes the reality that individuals are often faced with choices between activities and more or less desirable options (e.g. choosing between studying or going hiking with friends). Finally, effort cost indicates the consideration of whether the resources needed for the task are worth expending (Eccles and Wigfield, 2020). SEVT helps us understand some of the decision-making that underlies the motivation to cheat.

Situated Expectancy-Value Theory and Academic Integrity

Academic misconduct involves a moment where the student must decide whether to cheat or maintain academic integrity (Murdock and Anderman, 2006). Because cheating is a motivated behavior and students are faced with a decision to cheat or not, they may weigh their expectancy for success on a task with/without cheating. Furthermore, because subjective task values are more predictive of choices, students may consider the intrinsic, utility, and attainment value associated with a task. The extent to which a task is highly valued may play a role in the decision to cheat though expectancy for success or self-efficacy likely play roles as well (e.g. Lee et al., 2014). Costs could reasonably be expected to be part of this decision-making process as students determine whether the costs associated with not cheating (e.g. studying more and foregoing other activities) are worth the benefit (Murdock and Anderman, 2006).

Despite the prominence of SEVT in motivation research, few studies have empirically investigated the relationships between academic misconduct, expectancies for success, and/or task values. The extant research has mostly focused on frequencies of cheating behaviors; for example, studies have shown that when students are more interested in a subject (i.e. they hold intrinsic value for a subject) or find the content relevant (i.e. attainment value), they are less apt to cheat (Schraw et al., 2007).

Pavlin-Bernardic et al. (2017) examined the association between self-reported cheating in math (i.e. cheating to increase one's own success) versus cheating to help a peer be successful, and high school students' neutralizing attitudes and motivational beliefs, including goal orientations and task values. Cheating to help a peer was reported more frequently than cheating for one's personal benefit. However, cheating to help a peer be successful was not related to students' motivational beliefs whereas cheating for one's own success was significantly correlated with students' motivational beliefs. For instance, students' task values were negatively correlated with cheating behavior. Nevertheless, after controlling for prior achievement, goal orientations, and demographics, subjective task values and self-efficacy only explained an additional 1.3 percent of the variance in cheating. These findings suggest that task values played only a small role in students' cheating behaviors. Furthermore, it appears that the motivational beliefs associated with cheating may differ depending on whether cheating is done to increase one's own success versus peer success (Pavlin-Bernadic et al., 2017).

The aforementioned study utilized a composite score to assess task values though other studies have demonstrated that the different types of task values may have unique effects on academic conduct. For example, Lee et al. (2014) studied a sample of Korean students (speaking English as a second language) that reported high task values for English, low expectancies for success, and maladaptive strategy use (including cheating). Culture played an important role in cheating, indicating that culturally guided values, such as performing well in school, can interact with ability beliefs to influence cheating. They found that task values generally showed negative correlations with academic cheating, but neither intrinsic nor utility value significantly predicted cheating. The interaction between intrinsic value and self-efficacy was significant, whereas the interaction between utility value and self-efficacy approached significance. They concluded that the relationship between task values and cheating depended on students' self-efficacy: When students did not perceive that they could succeed at tasks that were highly valued, they were more likely to cheat (Lee et al., 2014).

While relatively underexplored as it pertains to academic misconduct, SEVT can nevertheless provide insight into students' cheating behaviors. In particular, task values, including cost, may be an especially fruitful area of future exploration, given the association between subjective task values and student choices (Wigfield and Eccles, 2000).

SELF-DETERMINATION THEORY

An interest in the basic needs that drive behavior goes back nearly as far as the discipline of psychology, with research by Abraham Maslow paving the way for scholars to question and study the idea that humans have needs that must be satisfied. Self-determination theory (SDT) is a result of that line of reasoning, with a focus being on students innate needs (Ryan and Deci, 2020).

SDT researchers have argued for three fundamental needs for which students are consistently striving, the fulfillment of which (or lack thereof) subsequently drives behavior (Deci and Ryan, 2004). The first need is *autonomy*, which concerns a sense of independence in one's actions (e.g. control over one's learning). The second need is *competence*, which concerns a perceived feeling of accomplishment and ability in a given domain (e.g. a student's sense of mastery in a course). The third need is *relatedness*, which refers to a perception of care and belonging in a given setting (e.g. a sense of instructor or peer support). One of the basic tenets of SDT is that satisfaction of the three fundamental needs will result in more autonomous (e.g. intrinsic) forms of motivation and more positive downstream behaviors, whereas; a lack of satisfaction, termed frustration, of any (or all) of the needs will result in more controlled (e.g. extrinsic) forms of motivation.

Self-Determination Theory and Academic Integrity

Since academic dishonesty is an inherently self-defeating enterprise with severe subsequent consequences and SDT argues that such outcomes are related to a frustration of needs, it is logical to argue that, according to SDT, cheating behaviors are a result of psychological need frustration. A lack of autonomy in the classroom may result in a feeling of frustration when faced with academic challenge or difficulty, with cheating being the only method of restoring some sense of control over the situation (e.g. a student can decide whether or not to cheat, which provides the needed sense of autonomy). A lack of competence may result in the student feeling that cheating is the only way to pass the class (e.g. a student does not feel capable enough to pass this class by working hard, so they have to cheat to get through). Finally, a lack of relatedness may result in disengagement with the classroom community and rules or even with the morality concerns that accompany inherently dishonest behaviors (e.g. a student does not feel cared for by the instructor, and therefore does not care about breaking the rules and feels justified in doing so despite how dishonest the behavior is).

This line of reasoning is supported by empirical evidence. For example, Kanat-Maymon et al. (2015) conducted two studies to determine if need satisfaction or frustration predicted the likelihood that Israeli middle-school and college students would cheat. The first study was a laboratory study that experimentally manipulated need satisfaction and need frustration along with a neutral condition. Participants who experienced need frustration were significantly more likely to cheat on a problem-solving and arithmetic task than participants who experienced need satisfaction or no experimental manipulation of needs (e.g. control condition). Their follow-up study with middle-schoolers found that autonomous motivation served as a mediator between needs satisfaction and academic dishonesty such that when needs were met, autonomous motivation was more likely to occur, which subsequently negatively predicted cheating.

Mih and Mih (2016) examined whether controlled motivation predicted self-reported cheating behaviors among Romanian high-school students. They argued that controlled motivation would be linked positively to procrastination, academic disengagement (termed disaffection), and fear of failure, which all positively predict maladaptive academic behaviors, and that these variables would serve as mechanisms between controlled motivation and academic dishonesty. Their results supported these hypotheses and also indicated that controlled motivation directly predicted self-reported cheating. Given the robust literature linking need satisfaction (or frustration) to subsequent motivation, like controlled or autonomous motivation (Ryan and Deci, 2020), these findings lend support to the importance of satisfying students' needs in an effort to reduce the incidence of academic dishonesty.

In a study of Belgian secondary students, Aelterman et al. (2019) found that students who did not internalize classroom rules (e.g. were motivated by more controlled forms of motivation) were more likely to defy classrooms rules and misbehave (including cheating on tests). Students who felt controlled in their classroom environments experienced pressure to assert their independence (e.g. autonomy frustration) by cheating on exams instead of working hard (e.g. competence frustration), without much care for their teachers' or peers' reactions (e.g. relatedness frustration).

Overall, the above summary suggests that SDT can provide a meaningful and powerful path forward for academic integrity researchers. It is clear that need satisfaction or frustration (and the subsequent forms of motivation that result), have significant impacts on the choices of students to engage in academic dishonesty.

MOVING THE RESEARCH FORWARD

Our review demonstrates that an array of motivation theories can be used to address academic dishonesty. Each of the aforementioned theories addresses a unique aspect of the academic motivation equation. For example, while AGT focuses on the goals that students hold when they engage with tasks, social-cognitive theory focuses on students' beliefs in their abilities to succeed at a task. And whereas attribution theory focuses on the effects of students' beliefs about why they succeeded or failed at a task, SDT focuses on the underlying intrinsic or extrinsic motivations that students hold for a task. In Table 1, we have summarized the primary motivational issues addressed by each theory, along with exemplars of implications for research on academic integrity.

Although a few studies of academic cheating have employed integrated theories of motivation (e.g. Anderman et al., 1998; Pavlin-Bernardic et al., 2017), this has not been the norm in research on academic integrity. Just as motivation is complex and can be best explained by multiple theories, academic cheating is also complex. If we want to truly understand the role that motivation plays in triggering academic misconduct, we need to consider incorporating multiple theoretical perspectives into future studies.

In recent years, some motivation scholars have suggested the benefits of integrating some of the primary motivation theories into a more comprehensive framework (e.g. Anderman, 2020; Dweck, 2017). Whereas the integration of these theories into a more comprehensive meta-theory may be a future development in the field, the application of multiple theories of motivation to studies of academic integrity in college populations will be an important next step for researchers.

Table 1 Motivation Theories and Implications for Research on Academic Integrity

Theory	Motivational Questions	Examples of Implications for Academic Integrity Research
Attribution Theory	After completion of a task, to what factors do students attribute their success or failure with the task?	Are students more likely to cheat if they attribute previous failures to a lack of ability?
Achievement Goal Theory	When students engage with academic tasks, is their primary goal to master the task or to demonstrate their ability?	Are students more likely to cheat if they are focused on demonstrating their ability relative to others on a task?
Situated Expectancy-Value Theory	Does the student expect to be successful with the task? Does the student find the task to be enjoyable, interesting, useful, and/or worth the time investment?	Are students less likely to cheat when they enjoy a task and believe it is useful?
Social Cognitive Theory	Does the student feel confident about engaging with the task?	Are students more likely to cheat when they do not feel confident in their ability to complete the task?
Self-Determination Theory	Is the student motivated to engage with the task for intrinsic or extrinsic reasons?	Are students more likely to cheat if they are focused on extrinsic outcomes (e.g. getting an "A")?

For example, suppose that a particular university is concerned with the high prevalence of cheating in biology courses. There are a number of avenues that researchers can pursue to examine this problem. For example, they might send anonymous surveys to students enrolled in biology classes, asking them how much they agree with various statements about their reasons for cheating.

When considering why students might cheat in biology, different students may report different reasons. Some might note that they cheat because they lack confidence in their abilities in biology (i.e. low self-efficacy); others might cheat because they have repeatedly done poorly in biology courses, and they attribute their poor performance to a lack of ability (attribution theory); and others might cheat because they are focused on either outperforming their peers or not appearing "dumb" compared to others (AGT). If the survey given to the students was framed in terms reflecting only one of the motivation theories reviewed in this chapter, the researchers might not ascertain the root causes of cheating at this university. Moreover, the researchers quite likely would find that the results indicate that there is diversity in students' reasons for cheating, and that this diversity varies based on student characteristics. For example, they might find that sophomores are more likely to cheat in biology because they do not find biology to be useful (i.e. SEVT), whereas seniors may be more likely to cheat in biology because they are focused on getting high test scores (i.e. SDT). Accounting for individual differences in motivational variables operationalized through varied frames of reference (in terms of expectations, perceived competences, goals, attributions, and needs) may add nuance to decoding factors guiding academic dishonesty.

IMPLICATIONS FOR PRACTICE

As suggested by Rettinger (2017), research on psychological factors, including motivation, offers recommendations to craft practices that promote academic integrity. Whereas the implications of this research for practice are vast (Anderman and Murdock, 2007), we focus here on implications for postsecondary contexts. We offer the following suggestions for college instructors and student affairs professionals who are interested in promoting academic integrity.

1. **Focus on mastery.** When instruction is designed so students are encouraged to master academic content, cheating will be less likely to occur (Bertram Gallant, 2017). Results of studies framed in AGT indicate that cheating occurs less often in classrooms that promote mastery (Miller et al., 2011; Van Yperen et al., 2011). The promotion of mastery in a college classroom might involve allowing students to make multiple attempts at assignments (without severe penalties).

2. **Avoid comparing students' performance.** Whereas it is tempting to display students' test scores so that everyone can see how they did compared to others, this virtually guarantees that students will perceive that classroom as being performance-oriented. Students who do not do well on such assignments may be particularly motivated to cheat, in order to avoid the embarrassment of being acknowledged as being less able than others. Moreover, when students observe that they scored poorly compared to others, their self-efficacy is likely to suffer, thus further increasing the likelihood of subsequent cheating.

3. **Don't focus exclusively on extrinsic outcomes.** Whereas testing and assessment are normal parts of instruction, students will be more likely to cheat when extrinsic outcomes are stressed. Instructors should avoid always talking about "the test." If possible, incorporate a variety of assessment strategies into a course, so that the outcome of any one assignment is not perceived as being extremely high-stakes. Moreover, encourage students to reflect on content that they have mastered, and the skills that they have gained, rather than only focusing on grades and test scores. Residence life staff in particular can play a critical role in helping students reflect on their progress and development rather than solely on test scores.

4. **Help students to become confident as they learn new material.** When students have high expectancies for success in a course or when they develop self-efficacy beliefs toward a topic, they are less likely to cheat. College instructors can help students to develop efficacy beliefs when courses are structured so that students focus on short-term goals (e.g. mastering one concept each week) and receive feedback that they have successfully achieved each short-term goal. For example, instructors can scaffold longer assignments to help students focus on short-term, achievable goals (e.g. by breaking a long assignment down into several manageable sub-components). When students focus on short-term goals and experience success, their self-efficacy will increase. In contrast, when students are focused on the end-goal (e.g. doing well on a high-stakes final exam), they often will feel anxious and not feel efficacious and, consequently, may be more likely to cheat. Moreover, student affairs professionals

can help students gain confidence by providing readily accessible study supports (e.g. access to quiet study areas; on-site evening tutoring for difficult courses; programming aimed at helping students to manage their time effectively).

5. **Help students make attributions to internal, controllable factors.** Provide students with feedback so that they can understand that when they have not done well on a particular assignment, it may be due to variables that are under their control. For example, if a student is given feedback showing the student that a problem was solved incorrectly because the student simply used the wrong strategy, then the student can learn from this mistake and will be more likely to be able to solve similar problems correctly in the future. In contrast, if students are not provided with feedback, students may attribute their incorrect solutions to a lack of ability ("I must be really bad at this"), and such beliefs may lead students to cheat in the future.

6. **Give students choices on assignment topics or due dates to bolster their feelings of autonomy.** Providing students with mandated assignments indicates higher levels of control on the part of the instructor and may stifle students' motivation, if they are not presented with choices. Allowing learners to have greater choice in assignment-prompts they are given, or the topics discussed in class, allows them to engage with knowledge they relate to at a deeper level. This may, in turn, lead them to develop intrinsically guided motivation for tasks, potentially reducing the incidence of dishonesty.

7. **Collaborate with students to create classroom expectations for academic integrity.** Instructors often provide

clear guidelines and expectations about academic dishonesty in their syllabi, and university administrators often provide clear guidelines in the institutions' academic integrity policies. However, interacting with students and reinforcing these expectations within diverse learning communities may help students develop a sense of care for their academic work, possibly contributing to lower rates of cheating. If students are able to connect academic integrity to a sense of community, they may be less likely to break this social contract through cheating.

8. **Foster supportive instructor–student relationships.** By establishing relationships with students based on mutual support and respect, instructors can create an environment in which cheating would be seen as damaging those relationships. Further, when students feel supported and cared for by instructors, they may be more willing to ask for help when struggling rather than turning to cheating to achieve their desired outcomes. Student affairs staff can promote these relationships by inviting faculty to conduct review sessions in residence halls or by providing students with vouchers that they can use to invite an instructor to join them for a meal.

9. **Help students see the value in what they are learning.** Emphasize the relevance, importance, or usefulness of the task. Encourage students to understand the connections between the content they are learning and their personal interests and goals. When students recognize that content is important, useful, or interesting, they are likely to hold higher value for it. Instructors can design assessment tasks that are more enjoyable (i.e. promote intrinsic value) and decrease

the potential social costs of failure (i.e. mitigate emotional cost) by providing low-stakes assessments or opportunities to revise. Student affairs staff can provide programming that helps students to relate their coursework to potential career opportunities.

CONCLUSION

In this chapter, we reviewed five prominent theories of motivation. We demonstrated that each of these theories addresses a unique aspect of motivation. Each theory has been used to frame studies of academic integrity. Whereas most studies have only incorporated one theory at a time, we note that future studies that incorporate multiple theories simultaneously will help scholars to better understand the multi-layered relationships between motivation and academic integrity. The extant research offers implications for practices aimed at promoting academic integrity, that can be adapted both by instructors and by student affairs professionals. Motivation theory and research helps us to identify the root causes of cheating and offer research-informed strategies that instructors can adopt to decrease the prevalence of cheating in college classrooms.

REFERENCES

Aelterman, N., Vansteenkiste, M. and Haerens, L. (2019). 'Correlates of students' internalization and defiance of classroom rules: A self-determination theory perspective', *British Journal of Educational Psychology, 89,* pp. 22–40.

Alt, D. (2015). 'Assessing the connection between self-efficacy for learning and justifying academic cheating in higher education learning environments', *Journal of Academic Ethics, 13,* pp. 77–90.

References

Anderman, E. M. (2020). 'Achievement motivation theory: Balancing precision and utility', *Contemporary Educational Psychology, 61.*

Anderman, E. M., Griesinger, T., and Westerfield, G. (1998). 'Motivation and cheating during early adolescence', *Journal of Educational Psychology, 90*, pp. 84–93.

Anderman, E. M. and Koenka, A. C. (2017). 'The relation between academic motivation and cheating', *Theory Into Practice, 56*(2), pp. 95–102.

Anderman, E. M. and Won, S. (2019). 'Academic cheating in disliked classes', *Ethics & Behavior, 29*(1), pp. 1–22.

Babaii, E. and Nejadghanbar, H. (2017). 'Plagiarism among Iranian graduate students of language studies: Perspectives and causes', *Ethics & Behavior, 27*, pp. 240–258.

Bandura, A. (1986). *Social foundations of thought and action: A social cognitive theory.* Englewood Cliffs, NJ: Prentice-Hall.

Bandura, A. (1997). *Self-efficacy: The exercise of control.* W.H. Freeman/Times Books/Henry Holt & Co.

Bardach, L., Oczlon, S., Pietschnig, J. and Lüftenegger, M. (2020). 'Has achievement goal theory been right? A meta-analysis of the relation between goal structures and personal achievement goals', *Journal of Educational Psychology, 112*(6), pp. 1197–1220.

Bertram Gallant, T. (2017). 'Academic Integrity as a Teaching & Learning Issue: From Theory to Practice', *Theory into Practice, 56*(2), pp. 88–94.

Bong, M. (2008). 'Effects of parent-child relationships and classroom goal structures on motivation, help-seeking avoidance, and cheating', *The Journal of Experimental Education, 76*(2), pp. 191–217.

Daumiller, M. and Janke, S. (2019). 'The impact of performance goals on cheating depends on how performance is evaluated', *AERA Open, 5*, pp. 1–10.

Deci, E. L. and Ryan, R. M. (Eds). (2004). *Handbook of self-determination research.* University of Rochester Press.

Dweck, C. S. (2017). 'From needs to goals and representations: Foundations for a unified theory of motivation, personality, and development', *Psychological Review*, *124*(6), pp. 689–719.

du Rocher, A. R. (2020). 'Active learning strategies and academic self-efficacy relate to both attentional control and attitudes towards plagiarism', *Active Learning in Higher Education*, *21*(3), pp. 203–216.

Eccles, J. S. and Wigfield, A. (2020). 'From expectancy-value theory to situated expectancy-value theory: A developmental, social cognitive, and sociocultural perspective on motivation', *Contemporary Educational Psychology*, *61*, 101859.

Elliot, A. J., Murayama, K. and Pekrun, R. (2011). 'A 3 × 2 achievement goal model', *Journal of Educational Psychology*, *103*(3), pp. 632–648.

Evans, E. D. and Craig, D. (1990a). 'Adolescent cognitions for academic cheating as a function of grade level and achievement status', *Journal of Adolescent Research*, *5*(3), pp. 325–345.

Evans, E. D. and Craig, D. (1990b). 'Teacher and student perceptions of academic cheating in middle and senior high schools', *The Journal of Educational Research*, *84*, pp. 44–53.

Fakouri, M. E. (1972). 'Achievement motivation and cheating', *Psychological Reports*, *31*(2), pp. 629–630.

Farnese M. L., Tramontano C., Fida, R. and Paciello M. (2011). 'Cheating behaviors in academic context: Does academic moral disengagement matter?', *Procedia—Social and Behavioral Sciences*, *29*, pp. 356–365.

Fida, R., Tramontano, C., Paciello, M., Ghezzi V. and Barbaranelli, C. (2018). 'Understanding the interplay among regulatory self-efficacy, moral disengagement, and academic cheating behaviour during vocational education: A three-wave study', *Journal of Business Ethics*, *153*, pp. 725–740.

Finn, K. V. and Frone, M. R. (2004) 'Academic performance and cheating: Moderating role of school Identification and self-efficacy', *The Journal of Educational Research*, *97*(3), pp. 115–121.

REFERENCES

Graham, S. (2020). 'An attributional theory of motivation', *Contemporary Educational Psychology*, *61*, 101861.

Harackiewicz, J. M., Barron, K. E., Pintrich, P. R., Elliot, A. J. and Thrash, T. M. (2002). 'Revision of achievement goal theory: Necessary and illuminating', *Journal of Educational Psychology*, *94*(3), pp. 638–645.

Harackiewicz, J. M. and Linnenbrink, E. A. (2005). 'Multiple Achievement Goals and Multiple Pathways for Learning: The Agenda and Impact of Paul R. Pintrich', *Educational Psychologist*, *40*(2), pp. 75–84.

Jordan, A. E. (2001). 'College student cheating: The role of motivation, perceived norms, attitudes, and knowledge of institutional policy', *Ethics & Behavior*, *11*, pp. 233–247.

Krou, M. R., Fong, C. J. and Hoff, M. A. (2020). 'Achievement motivation and academic dishonesty: A meta-analytic investigation', *Educational Psychology Review*.

Kanat-Maymon, Y., Benjamin, M., Stavsky, A., Shoshani, A. and Roth, G. (2015). 'The role of basic need fulfillment in academic dishonesty: A self-determination theory perspective', *Contemporary Educational Psychology*, 43, pp. 1–9. doi: 10.1016/j.cedpsych.2015.08.002:

Kaplan, A., Middleton, M. J., Urdan, T. and Midgley, C. (2002). 'Achievement goals and goal structures', *Goals, goal structures, and patterns of adaptive learning*, pp. 21–53.

Lee, J., Bong, M. and Kim, S. (2014). 'Interaction between task values and self-efficacy on maladaptive achievement strategy use', *Educational Psychology*, *34*(5), pp. 538–560.

Lee, S. D., Kuncel, N. R. and Gau, J. (2020). 'Personality, attitude, and demographic correlates of academic dishonesty: A meta-analysis', *Psychological Bulletin*, *146*(11), pp. 1042–1058.

Marsden, H., Carroll, M. and Neill, J. T. (2005). 'Who cheats at university? A self-report study of dishonest academic behaviours in a sample of Australian university students', *Australian Journal of Psychology*, *57*, pp. 1–10.

Mih, C. and Mih, V. (2016). 'Fear of failure, disaffection and procrastination as mediators between controlled motivation and academic
cheating', *Cognition, Brain, Behavior. An Interdisciplinary Journal, 20,*
pp. 117–132.

Miller, A., Shoptaugh, C. and Wooldridge, J. (2011). 'Reasons not to
cheat, academic-integrity responsibility, and frequency of cheating', *The Journal of Experimental Education, 79,* pp. 169–184.

Murdock, T. B. and Anderman, E. M. (2006). 'Motivational perspectives on student cheating: Toward an integrated model of academic dishonesty', *Educational Psychologist, 41,* 129–145.

Murdock, T. B., Beauchamp, A. S. and Hinton, A. M. (2008). 'Predictors
of cheating and cheating attributions: Does classroom context
influence cheating and blame for cheating?', *European Journal of
Psychology of Education, 23,* 477–492.

Murdock, T. B., Hale, N. M. and Weber, M. J. (2001). 'Predictors of
cheating among early adolescents: Academic and social motivations', *Contemporary Educational Psychology, 26,* pp. 96–115.

Murdock, T. B., Miller, A. D. and Goetzinger, A. (2007). 'Effects of
classroom context on university students' judgments about cheating: Mediating and moderating processes', *Social Psychology of
Education, 10,* pp. 141–169.

Nora, W. L. Y. and Zhang, K. C. (2010). 'Motives of cheating among
secondary students: the role of self-efficacy and peer influence',
Asia Pacific Education Review, 11, pp. 573–584.

Ogilvie, J. and Stewart, A. (2010). 'The integration of rational choice
and self-efficacy theories: A situational analysis of student misconduct', *Australian and New Zealand Journal of Criminology, 43*(1),
pp. 130–155.

Park, S. (2020). 'Goal contents as predictors of academic cheating in
college students', *Ethics & Behavior, 30*(8), pp. 628–639.

Pavlin-Bernardic, N., Rovan, D. and Pavlovic, J. (2017). 'Academic
cheating in mathematics classes: A motivational perspective',
Ethics & Behavior, 27(6), pp. 486–501.

Pintrich, P. R. (2000). 'Multiple goals, multiple pathways: The role of goal orientation in learning and achievement', *Journal of Educational Psychology*, *92*(3), pp. 544–555. **https://doi-10.1037/0022-0663.92.3.544**

Pulfrey, C. J., Vansteenkiste, M. and Michou, A. (2019). 'Achievement goal complex and cheating: Both the goals we set and the way we set them matter!', *Frontiers in Psychology*, *10*.

Rettinger, D. A. (2017). 'The role of emotions and attitudes in causing and preventing cheating', *Theory into Practice*, *56*, pp. 103–110.

Ring, C. and Kavussanu, M. (2018). 'The impact of achievement goals on cheating in sport', *Psychology of Sport and Exercise*, *35*, pp. 98–103.

Ryan, R. M. and Deci, E. L. (2020). 'Intrinsic and extrinsic motivation from a self-determination theory perspective: Definitions, theory, practices, and future directions', *Contemporary Educational Psychology*, *61*, p. 101860.

Schraw, G., Olafson, L., Kuch, F., Lehman, T., Lehman, S. and McCrudden, M. T. (2007). 'Interest and academic cheating'. In E. M. Anderman and T. B. Murdock (Eds), *Psychology of Academic Cheating* (pp. 59–77). Elsevier Academic Press.

Stephens, J. M. (2017). 'How to Cheat and Not Feel Guilty: Cognitive Dissonance and its Amelioration in the Domain of Academic Dishonesty', *Theory Into Practice*, *56*(2), pp. 111–120.

Stephens, J. M. and Gehlbach, H. (2007). 'Under pressure and underengaged: Motivational profiles and academic cheating in high school'. In *Psychology of Academic Cheating* (pp. 107–134). Academic Press.

Treasure, D. C., Duda, J. L., Hall, H. K., Roberts, G. C., Ames, C., & Maehr, M. L. (2001). Clarifying misconceptions and misrepresentations in achievement goal research in sport: A response to Harwood, Hardy, and Swain', *Journal of Sport and Exercise Psychology*, *23*(4), pp. 317–329.

Urdan, T. and Kaplan, A. (2020). 'The origins, evolution, and future directions of achievement goal theory', *Contemporary Educational Psychology, 61*, p. 101862.

Usher, E. L. and Pajares, F. (2008). 'Self-efficacy for self-regulated learning: A validation study', *Educational and Psychological Measurement, 68*(3), pp. 443–463.

Van Yperen, N. W., Hamstra, M. R., and van der Klauw, M. (2011). 'To win, or not to lose, at any cost: The impact of achievement goals on cheating', *British Journal of Management, 22*, pp. S5–S15.

Weiner, B. (1990). 'History of motivational research in education', *Journal of Educational Psychology, 82*, pp. 616–622.

Weiner, B. (1996). 'Searching for order in social motivation', *Psychological Inquiry, 7*, pp. 199–216.

Whitley, B. E. (1998). 'Factors associated with cheating among college students: A review', *Research in Higher Education, 39*(3), pp. 235–274.

Wigfield, A. and Eccles, J. S. (2000). 'Expectancy-value theory of achievement motivation', *Contemporary Educational Psychology, 25*, pp. 68–81.

Wigfield, A. and Koenka, A. C. (2020). 'Where do we go from here in academic motivation theory and research? Some reflections and recommendations for future work', *Contemporary Educational Psychology, 61,* p. 101872.

CHAPTER 5

The Moral Puzzle of Academic Cheating: Perceptions, Evaluations, and Decisions

Talia Waltzer and Audun Dahl

University of California, Santa Cruz

Our research on academic integrity began with two puzzling facts. First, cheating is common. The vast majority of students cheat during their academic careers (McCabe et al., 2012; Stephens, 2018; Waltzer & Dahl). Second, to most people, cheating is wrong. Nearly everyone appears to agree that academic cheating is unfair, dishonest, harmful, and morally bad (see, for example, Gert, 2004; Green, 2006; Miller et al., 2011). Hence the puzzle: How can cheating be at once so common and so universally condemned? How can there be such an apparent gap between actions and judgments? One possibility is that moral judgments have little bearing on decisions about cheating. This is indeed what many scientists have concluded. In reviewing the literature, McCabe (1997) concluded that "morality does not seem to be a major influence on student decisions to cheat or not to cheat" (p. 444). Another possibility, advocated by this chapter, is that moral judgments do play a crucial role in students' decisions about cheating, and that the gap between judgments and actions is far smaller than often assumed.

We propose that a key to the puzzle of cheating lies in recognizing that *perceptions, evaluations,* and *decisions* about cheating vary dramatically from one situation to another (Dahl & Waltzer, 2018; Miller et al., 2007; Rettinger, 2007; Rettinger & Kramer, 2009; Waltzer & Dahl, in press). Simply put, in most situations, students accurately perceive cheating, judge that cheating is wrong, and decide to refrain from cheating (Kohlberg, 1971; Levine et al., 2010; Rundle et al., 2019; Turiel, 2003). In some situations, however, students either cheat because they perceive cheating inaccurately, deem that cheating is acceptable, or decide to prioritize other pressing concerns over their concerns with academic integrity. This chapter proposes that students' judgments about cheating closely align with their decisions about cheating and that the gaps between actions and judgments are small, rare, and predictable.

We begin this chapter by defining cheating and reviewing alternative theoretical accounts of the cheating puzzle. After considering some limitations of these accounts, we will introduce our account of situational perceptions, evaluations, and decisions about cheating. We will review evidence for how each of these three steps shape student cheating. In the concluding section, we consider how perceptions, evaluations, and decisions about cheating develop during students' academic careers and may be targeted by interventions that strengthen academic integrity (Bertram Gallant, 2011; Bretag, 2020).

ACADEMIC CHEATING: WHAT, WHEN, AND WHY? WHAT IS CHEATING?

We define academic cheating as a violation of academic rules that is intended to yield an academic advantage to persons involved. This distinguishes cheating from other school violations such as student conduct violations (e.g., violence, underage drinking), which are not intended to yield academic advantages. Of course, a given act of cheating may fail to yield an academic advantage, for instance, because the cheater is caught. Still, what matters for our definition is that the student completed the cheating act with the expectation—however misguided—that they would be better off academically than if they had not completed that act.

Note that we do not define cheating as an unfair or otherwise immoral action (for alternative definitions, see Green, 2006; Murdock et al., 2016). This is because we seek a psychological definition for an empirical research agenda (Dahl & Waltzer, 2018). Terms such as "unfair" or "morally wrong" are not empirical concepts with scientific methods. They are instead evaluative concepts over which psychologists have no special authority. Insofar as we discuss notions of "morally wrong" or "unfair" in this paper, we are referring to what certain individuals *consider to be* morally wrong or unfair. It is true that most people consider cheating and dishonesty to be generally wrong, but—as we will see—there are also situations in which most people judge cheating or lying to be okay (e.g., Freeman et al., 1999; Perkins & Turiel, 2007).

WHEN DOES CHEATING HAPPEN?

The variability in definitions of cheating and in the academic rules violated can make it difficult to measure how often students cheat. Still, there is no doubt that a large majority of students—likely more than 90 percent—cheat at least once during their academic careers (Curtis & Vardanega, 2016; McCabe et al., 2012; Waltzer & Dahl, in press). At the same time, it appears that most students also refrain from cheating on most of their assignments (Levine et al., 2010; Rundle et al., 2019). In one unpublished survey from our lab, undergraduates ($N = 227$) reported that they had cheated on less than 5% of their recent assignments (as assessed by whether they were at least 50% confident about having cheated, Waltzer et al., 2019). This fits with research on non-academic dishonesty, which suggests that, on average, people lie once or twice a day, a vanishingly small number considering the countless interactions they have daily (DePaulo et al., 1996; Levine et al., 2010; Serota et al., 2010). Like getting married, academic cheating has a high lifetime prevalence but a low daily frequency for any one individual. It is common at the level of individuals yet rare at the level of situations.

WHY STUDY CHEATING? ITS PRACTICAL AND THEORETICAL SIGNIFICANCE

When cheating does happen, it has major consequences for students and their institutions. Students who cheat are at risk of missed learning opportunities, inadequate preparation for future work, failing grades, and even barred enrollment (Bertram Gallant & Stephens, 2020; Cizek, 2003; Russell, 2014). Cheating can make it harder for non-cheating students to get good grades, especially in classes that grade students on a curve. In the aggregate, cheating can also undermine trust in academic degrees and heighten the workload and frustrations of instructors and administrators (Bertram Gallant, 2011; Chace, 2012). For these reasons, many students, instructors, administrators, and educational scholars have sought ways to reduce cheating.

Cheating has also been a focus in research on moral development and moral psychology (Ariely, 2012; Drake, 1941; Hartshorne & May, 1928; Kohlberg, 1971; Stephens, 2018; Zhao et al., 2019; Zhao et al., in press). Cheating has been particularly theoretically significant because it is widely condemned, very common, and relatively easy to elicit in laboratory studies with both children and adults. It has, thus, become a notorious illustration of the so-called "judgment-action gap": Most people judge cheating to be wrong yet sometimes decide to cheat (Blasi, 1980; Stephens, 2018). In the words of Stephens (2018), "[t]here is often a divide between that which we say we ought do—or not do—and that which we do. Many students, for example, cheat, even when they believe it is wrong to do so" (p. 2). This apparent gap has led many scholars to conclude that moral judgments do not guide students' decisions about cheating (e.g., Brown, 2002; Haines et al., 1986; Houston, 1976, Lee et al., 2020; McCabe et al., 2012).

PRIOR THEORETICAL APPROACHES TO CHEATING AND THE JUDGMENT-ACTION GAP

In the prior literature on academic cheating, we have observed two theoretical responses to the judgment-action gap. One approach proposes that people readily disregard, or *neutralize*, their moral principles against cheating. In the words of Haines and colleagues (1986), students use neutralization techniques "before, during, or after deviant behavior to deflect the disapproval of others and self" (p. 344; see also Bandura, 2016; Stephens & Nicholson, 2008). Hence, it is proposed, moral principles against cheating have little bearing on whether people decide to cheat, since these principles can readily be neutralized to avoid feeling bad about one's actions. The second theoretical approach begins with the assumption that moral principles do not reliably keep people from cheating, but that it is possible to predict cheating from characteristics of individuals or their institutions, such as personality traits, academic performance, or the presence of honor codes. We will briefly discuss these two theoretical approaches before introducing our own view.

Neutralization Accounts of Cheating. Many scholars have explained the judgment-action gap by proposing that students neutralize, or rationalize, their acts of cheating (Haines et al., 1986; McCabe et al., 2012; for related accounts, see Ariely, 2012; Bandura, 2016). Neutralization and rationalization refer to techniques by which students render otherwise wrong actions acceptable so that they can engage in those actions without feeling bad. Denial of responsibility or appeals to higher loyalties are but two examples of neutralization techniques (Sykes & Matza, 1957). Haines and colleagues (1986) wrote that neutralization techniques "free the individual to deviate without considering himself or herself a deviant, thus eliminating or reducing the sense of guilt or wrongdoing" (p. 346; see Bandura, 2016). That is, according to neutralization approaches, students neutralize their cheating not because they genuinely think cheating is acceptable but, for instance, because they want to cheat without feeling bad about it.

How do we distinguish neutralization from genuine moral reasoning? That is, when are students neutralizing their cheating acts to avoid feeling bad about themselves and when are they reasoning that cheating would be okay regardless of their personal involvement? It turns out that this question has received very little attention in research on neutralization and related concepts (Dahl & Waltzer, 2018, 2020). It is often assumed that any acceptance of acts of cheating must involve neutralization. However, virtually everyone thinks it is sometimes okay to violate a general moral principle to uphold something more important (Turiel & Dahl, 2019). Most people judge, for instance, that it can be okay to sacrifice the life of one person to protect the lives of others (Dahl et al., 2018). Freeman and colleagues (1999) found that most physicians thought it was okay to lie to insurance companies if such deception was necessary to get coverage for life-saving surgery. (By contrast, physicians rarely accepted deception to cover non-essential procedures, such as cosmetic surgery.) Many other studies have shown that children, adolescents, and adults think it is sometimes okay to lie, for instance, to protect one's welfare or rights (Gingo, 2017; Jensen et al., 2004; Perkins & Turiel, 2007). Thus, the finding that students think cheating is sometimes okay does not by itself demonstrate neutralization.

A second limitation of neutralization approaches is that they do not readily explain why cheating and other forms of dishonesty are rare compared to acts of academic integrity and honesty (Levine et al., 2010; Rundle et al., 2019). If people can neutralize cheating whenever it suits their self-interest, why do students cheat on so few assignments and, as we will note, primarily when they face strong situational pressures? Moreover, even when students do cheat, they often feel conflicted and even guilty about their actions (Dahl & Waltzer, 2018; Stephens & Nicholson, 2008). Contrary to the neutralization account, we will propose that judgments about right and wrong play a decisive role in student cheating.

Individual and Institutional Accounts of Cheating. Instead of examining the psychological processes that lead students to cheat in specific situations (e.g., moral judgments or neutralization), other approaches have sought to predict rates of cheating from individual and institutional characteristics. For example, McCabe and colleagues (2001) wrote that "both individual and contextual factors influence cheating [. . .] In addition, an institution's academic integrity programs and policies [. . .] can have a significant influence on students' behavior." (p. 219). This body of research has found correlations between rates of cheating and student characteristics, such as GPA (Bunn et al., 1992; Whitley, 1998), gender (Teixeira & Rocha, 2010), international student status (Beasley, 2016; Bertram Gallant et al., 2015), orientations toward academic mastery/performance (Anderman & Midgley, 2004), and conscientiousness (Giluk & Postlethwaite, 2014; Lee et al., 2020). At the institutional level, scholars have predicted rates of cheating based on academic major or use of honor codes (Baird, 1980; McCabe et al., 2012).

These approaches have advanced our knowledge about the individual and institutional conditions under which cheating is more likely. Still, by definition, general individual and institutional characteristics cannot be used to predict situational variability in cheating, since the same student within the same institution will decide to cheat on one assignment but not another. Even students in "high-risk" groups refrain from cheating on many, if not most, assignments. And even students in "low-risk" groups cheat (Galloway, 2012; Jordan, 2001; Rettinger & Jordan, 2005).

We are not the first to call for a psychological account of why students cheat in some situations and not others

(Bertram Gallant & Stephens, 2020; Bretag, 2020; Hodgkinson et al., 2016; Ogilvie & Stewart, 2010; Rettinger, 2007). Miller and colleagues (2007) wrote that "instead of asking 'who cheats?' perhaps we should ask 'when and why do some students cheat?'" (p. 29). More recently, Lee and colleagues (2020) called for research on "students across semesters where the situational influence of within-person differences in academic work load and extracurricular demands could be examined" (p. 1052). In the following sections, we outline the core tenets and key evidence of a situational and moral-psychological account of why students cheat.

A SITUATIONAL AND MORAL-PSYCHOLOGICAL ACCOUNT OF ACADEMIC CHEATING: PERCEPTIONS, EVALUATIONS, AND DECISIONS

To examine the relation between situated judgments and decisions about cheating, this chapter takes a new approach to the moral puzzle of cheating. Our approach draws on advances in research on moral psychology and moral development (Killen & Dahl, 2021; Turiel & Dahl, 2019). We build our approach from three key insights.

First, *perceptions* of facts—for instance, about whether a teacher has in fact prohibited collaboration on a given assignment—shape evaluative judgments about right and wrong (Wainryb, 1991; Wainryb et al., 2004). Such perceptions, sometimes called informational assumptions, determine how individuals apply moral or other principles to a situation under evaluation. For instance, in one study, people who believed that corporal punishment is detrimental for a child's healthy development tended to judge corporal punishment as wrong (Wainryb, 1991). But when the same people were asked to imagine that corporal punishment had been beneficial for children's development because it helped them learn, participants' evaluations became more positive. This work illustrates how judgments about right and wrong build on perceptions about matters of fact.

Second, people form *evaluations* by incorporating multiple and sometimes competing principles, such as principles about protecting rights, promoting welfare, and being honest (Dahl et al., 2018; Nucci et al., 2017; Waytz et al., 2013). For instance, when evaluating whether it is okay to harm another person, children and adults consider not only the immediate harm and rights of that person but also further ramifications, such as how the act may save others (Dahl et al., 2018; Fiske & Rai, 2014; Jambon & Smetana, 2014; Nucci et al., 2017). Under some circumstances, most people judge that it is okay to harm others to prevent a greater harm (Dahl et al., 2018).

Third, such evaluations guide but do not fully determine *decisions* about what to do (Ajzen & Fishbein, 2005; Lee et al., 2021; Turiel, 2003). Research on attitudes has shown that attitudes about specific situations, say, whether it is good to cheat under some specified circumstances, predict actions in those situations (Ajzen & Fishbein, 2005). Of course, positive and negative evaluations do not fully determine actions. Occasionally, people act in ways they judge to be wrong. Still, instances of judgment-action contradictions appear to be the exception rather than the rule. In the case of cheating, we propose that individuals make such exceptions when they believe cheating is only a little wrong or that refraining from cheating will have unbearably high personal costs.

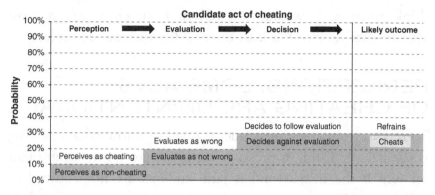

Figure 1

Note: By candidate act of cheating, we mean an act that (a) an individual is otherwise motivated to carry out that (b) would, if completed, meet the criteria for cheating. The vertical axis represents the cumulative probability of actions. The height of each box is meant for illustration only. If the probabilities were as depicted in this graph, this would represent a situation with unusually high risk (30%) of cheating (10% chance of failed perception, 10% chance of evaluating cheating as wrong, and 10% chance of deciding to cheat despite evaluating it as wrong). The graph illustrates a high degree of correspondence between perceptions and evaluations and between evaluations and decisions. For instance, there is only a 10% chance the person will act against their evaluation and a 90% chance the person will act in accordance with their evaluation. Lastly, each link in the model is probabilistic, not deterministic: There are cases, for instance, in which students evaluate cheating as okay and nevertheless decide to refrain from cheating because of other concerns, such as fear of being caught. These further factors are not represented in this schematic figure.

Below, we review evidence for the role of situated perceptions, evaluations, and decisions in student cheating (Figure 1). Each of the three components respond to situational features, undergo developmental change, and create opportunities for interventions aimed at strengthening academic integrity. Jointly, these psychological components help explain why most students think cheating is wrong and refrain from cheating on most assignments yet cheat at least once in their academic careers.

PERCEPTIONS: SOME ACTS OF CHEATING ARE UNINTENTIONAL

To refrain from cheating, students need to know what cheating is (Waltzer & Dahl, in press). Imagine a take-home assignment on which the instructor has said students are not allowed to collaborate. If a student wrongly believes they are permitted, or even encouraged, to collaborate on the assignment, the student has no reason to decline a peer's suggestion to work together. Similarly, if the student tries to avoid collaborating but does not know what entails collaboration in that class, they can still end up unintentionally cheating. To explain why the student decided to cheat, it is essential to consider the student's failure to perceive collaboration as cheating.

Students' perceptions shape decisions to cheat because students generally evaluate cheating as wrong, and they typically decide to avoid it as we will see more in the subsequent sections. For instance, students are far more likely to judge an act as wrong if they perceive it as cheating (Waltzer & Dahl, in press; Waltzer et al., 2018; Modi et al., 2021). One study found that when students perceived a text as plagiarized, they judged it as wrong 90% of the time compared to 6% for texts not perceived as plagiarism (Waltzer & Dahl, in press).

Despite the likely role of perceptions in many cheating decisions, little past research on cheating has considered students' perceptions. Often, researchers assess cheating by asking students whether they have cheated or by observing behaviors that the researchers perceive as cheating (for discussions, see Ashworth et al., 1997; Barnhardt, 2016). Neither of these approaches assesses whether research participants share instructors' or researchers' perceptions of which acts constitute cheating.

There is growing evidence that many acts of cheating happen because students fail to perceive those acts as cheating. Several studies have shown that students and instructors often disagree widely in their perceptions of cheating (Childers & Bruton, 2016; Roig, 1997, 2001; Waltzer & Dahl, in press). For instance, in one study, approximately half of students did not think paraphrased passages of text without citations counted as plagiarism even though professors agreed that they were plagiarized (Roig, 1997). Similarly, interviews with students about their own past experiences with cheating suggest that many students are unaware or uncertain about whether they are cheating (Ashworth et al., 2003; Modi et al., 2021; Power, 2009; Stephens & Nicholson, 2008; Waltzer et al., 2018). In research with engineering and social science students, we asked students to describe a prior situation in which they had cheated (Modi et al., 2021; Waltzer et al., 2018). Less than half of students said they had known they were cheating at the time of the action, suggesting that perceptions may play a crucial role in student cheating.

It is possible, of course, that students sometimes falsely claim they did not realize they were cheating so that they can present themselves favorably to researchers. Still, this is unlikely to explain all of the cases in which students claim not to have known they were cheating. First, if students merely wanted to present themselves in a positive light, they could have simply said they did not cheat. In contrast, we have found that most students readily describe prior acts of cheating (Waltzer et al., 2018; Waltzer et al., 2019). Second, as we saw, studies of cheating perceptions have revealed considerable disagreement among teachers and students about what constitutes cheating (Roig, 1997, 2001; Waltzer & Dahl, in press). Given such disagreements, it is almost inevitable that students will sometimes cheat without perceiving their acts as cheating.

Students' confusion about what constitutes cheating can arise from differences in academic cultures and traditions. For instance, different academic disciplines conceptualize plagiarism differently (Bidgood & Merrill, 2017; Borg, 2009) and views on authorship and originality can vary across cultural communities and educational backgrounds (Ashworth et al., 2003; Chou, 2010; Pennycook, 1996). For instance, this may place international students at particular risk for unintentional cheating (Hayes & Introna, 2005; Park, 2003).

Even more directly, instructional experiences likely contribute to students' ability to perceive cheating accurately. Students often rely on their instructors as a primary source of information on what constitutes academic integrity (Gullifer & Tyson, 2014; Husain et al., 2017; Sun & Hu, 2020). However, some research suggests that teachers rarely discuss cheating or integrity in their classrooms, and what rare discussions they do have mostly focus on threats of punishment (Bareket-Shavit et al., 2018). With widely varying expectations across institutions, disciplines, and even classes and few explicit conversations about what is allowed in a particular class, students are often left to rely on their own assumptions of what is allowed. This could make it difficult to bring everyone onto the same page about what academic integrity means in each classroom.

In summary, perceptions play an essential role in decisions to cheat. People incorporate their beliefs about facts of the world to evaluate actions and decide what to do (Wainryb, 1991). Students can only choose to refrain from cheating if they first *perceive* an act as cheating. In many cases, far from illustrating a judgment–action gap, students do not even believe they are cheating. Still, the perception step is often overlooked, as many educators assume students already know what counts as cheating. In the next section, we turn to the question of how students evaluate acts they do perceive as cheating.

EVALUATIONS: PEOPLE DEEM CHEATING ACCEPTABLE IN SOME CIRCUMSTANCES

To understand the role of evaluations in academic cheating, we consider two concurrent points. First, nearly all students judge that cheating is generally wrong. Second, most people evaluate cheating and other forms of dishonesty as okay under some circumstances. We will discuss evidence for each point in turn.

Numerous studies now show that students generally care about academic integrity and think cheating is wrong (Ashworth et al., 2003; Davis et al., 1992; Modi et al., 2021; Stephens, 2018; Waltzer et al., 2021). In a large internal survey of undergraduates at our university ($N = 1,110$), 83% of students said academic integrity was "important" or "very important" to them. Similarly, studies tend to find over 90% of students say cheating is wrong (Davis et al., 1992; Waltzer & Dahl, in press). Common reasons students give for why they think cheating is wrong include concerns about learning, fairness, and intellectual property (Modi et al., 2021; Waltzer & Dahl, in press; Waltzer et al., 2018). Thus, contrary to some suggestions, most students do not generally view cheating as a moral "gray area" (McCabe et al., 2012, p. 8). Students' concerns for academic integrity, thus, generally provide a motivation for refraining from cheating.

At the same time, however, students judge cheating to be more acceptable under certain circumstances. Some opportunities to cheat pit concerns with academic integrity against morality, loyalty, or other important concerns. Students are sometimes asked by a peer to share their homework answers (Waltzer et al., 2018). If the peer is unable to complete required homework on their own, the student faces a dilemma that pits academic integrity against concerns with both loyalty and their friends' academic survival in the class. We have found that students evaluate hypothetical acts of cheating that involve such realistic, competing concerns more positively than straightforward acts of cheating, in which such concerns are absent (Samuelson et al., 2021). For instance, if a hypothetical student faces unfair treatment by the instructor or family obligations that prevent them from completing the assignment, participants tend to judge that it is far more acceptable to cheat (DeBernardi et al., 2021; Jensen et al., 2002).

Studies of students' evaluations of hypothetical acts of cheating are critical because, in these studies, students face no pressure to defend their actions. Some scholars have suggested that students may evaluate their own violations positively to maintain a positive self-image (e.g., Bandura, 2016). This explanation cannot account for why students also think that it is okay for other people to cheat in hypothetical events involving unfamiliar individuals. Findings on evaluations of hypothetical events involving unfamiliar others, thus, suggest that students genuinely deem cheating as acceptable in some situations.

Though evaluations of hypothetical cheating are particularly telling, similar processes of evaluation are also evident in students' own decisions about cheating. Students sometimes judge that the circumstances, such as exceptional pressures, rendered their acts of cheating more acceptable, and they often express conflict and guilt about their cheating actions (Dahl & Waltzer, 2018; Modi et al., 2021; Waltzer et al., 2018). For example, in one study, participants who copied in a lab task reported increased guilt afterward (e.g., "[t]aking credit for someone else's work made me feel guilty," Waltzer et al., 2018). These expressions of guilt and conflict point to students' deep and persistent concerns with academic integrity, even in situations when they decide to cheat (Turiel & Dahl, 2019).

In summary, students overwhelmingly think cheating is wrong, and this negative evaluation provides one consistent reason not to cheat. Still, a concern for honesty and integrity is not the only evaluative consideration at work. Some situations pit concerns with academic integrity against competing concerns (e.g., loyalty, others' welfare), forcing students to prioritize one concern over another. In some such conflicted situations, students may choose cheating as the "lesser of two evils" (Hallborg, 1997). In the next section, we will discuss how evaluations guide decisions about cheating.

DECISIONS: UNDER CERTAIN PRESSURES, STUDENTS SOMETIMES CHEAT DESPITE JUDGING CHEATING AS WRONG

Like the prior section on evaluations, this section on decisions will make two points that exist in some tension. Our first point will be that evaluations exert a heavy pressure on decisions about cheating, leading students to act in accordance with their evaluations most of the time. Our second point will be that, when faced with certain pressures and high personal stakes, students sometimes decide to cheat even when they judge cheating to be wrong.

In most situations, students act in accordance with their judgments against cheating. In nearly all cases, students evaluate cheating as wrong and, accordingly, refrain from cheating (Curtis & Vardanega, 2016; Levine et al., 2010; Rundle et al., 2019; Waltzer et al., 2019). As mentioned, students appear to cheat on fewer than 5% of assignments (Waltzer et al., 2019; see also Karlins et al., 1988). Moreover, when students do cheat, they are more likely to do so in situations where they evaluate cheating more positively. Students' own estimates of how likely they are to cheat in a situation are strongly correlated with their evaluations of cheating in that situation (DeBernardi et al., 2021). Moreover, as noted in the prior section, students are more likely to deem cheating acceptable in the kinds of situations in which they tend to cheat, for instance, when faced with exceptional pressures (Samuelson et al., 2021; Waltzer et al., 2018).

Of course, evaluations are not the only forces that shape students' decisions to cheat. In addition to their concern that cheating is simply wrong, students also refrain from cheating out of concerns for their own learning, risks of consequences, and if they think it is feasible to complete the assignment without cheating (Waltzer et al., 2019; see also McLeod & Simkin, 2010; Miller et al., 2011; Rundle et al., 2020).

Occasionally, however, students do decide to act against their evaluations by cheating despite evaluating the act as wrong. We propose that these situations are rare, compared to the number of situations in which students refrain from cheating, and predictable. The factors that predict such situations seem to resemble the factors that predict students' positive evaluations of cheating, such as thinking they do not have enough time, not knowing how to pass the assignment without cheating, or feeling pressured to help someone else (McLeod & Simkin, 2010; Modi et al., 2021; Stephens & Nicholson, 2008; Waltzer et al., 2018). Moreover, students are more likely to cheat when performance outcomes (e.g., obtaining a top score) are emphasized over learning and mastery (Jordan, 2001; Lang, 2013; Murdock et al., 2004). Other scholars have noted that higher-pressure contexts, such as competitive majors, push students to cheat more (Bertram Gallant et al., 2015; McCabe & Treviño, 1995).

In short, it seems that students typically act in accordance with their evaluations of cheating. Most of the time, students view cheating as wrong and, accordingly, refrain from cheating. In some situations, for instance when facing exceptional pressures, students deem cheating as more acceptable and decide to cheat. In a small number of situations, students face conflicts that involve high personal stakes (e.g., feeling desperate for a certain grade) that lead them to cheat despite judging that cheating is wrong. Since these situations are so infrequent, they do not undermine our claim that evaluations generally guide decisions about cheating. Still, students' decisions to cheat, whenever they happen, can have major consequences for individuals and institutions and, hence, warrant the kind of scientific examination that we have proposed in this chapter.

CONCLUSION

We started this chapter with the puzzle of why cheating is at once very common yet widely condemned. We propose that a psychological account of students' *perceptions*, *evaluations*, and *decision-making* can help explain why and when students cheat, as well as why and when they refrain from cheating. When analyzed at the level of situational decision-making, the evidence suggests that moral judgments play a major role in whether students cheat (Killen & Dahl, 2021; Waltzer & Dahl, in press). We argued that students act in accordance with their judgments most of the time, either by refraining from cheating when they think cheating is wrong or cheating when they think cheating is okay.

Our framework raises key questions for future research on why students cheat. Far more research is needed on how students learn to perceive cheating, under which circumstances they evaluate cheating as acceptable, and when they decide to cheat despite judging that cheating is wrong. Beyond this research on perceptions, evaluations, and decisions about specific acts of cheating, further research is also needed on the development of cheating across adolescence and early adulthood. The frequency of cheating peaks early in college and decreases in later years according to both self-report and other measures (Bertram Gallant et al., 2015; Haines et al., 1986; Olafson et al., 2014; Whitley, 1998). Such changes in cheating rates likely reflect developmental changes in students' perceptions, evaluations, and decision-making about cheating. These changes occur, in part, through encounters with peers, teachers, and traditions at different academic institutions. Children do not enter school with knowledge of norms about ownership and integrity, but must develop such norms over time (Olson & Shaw, 2010). In moving beyond individual-level questions about "who cheats," it will be important to study both situational and developmental variability in cheating.

Our proposed situational model of student cheating also points to multiple paths for intervention. Since decisions about cheating involve multiple components, interventions may need to be similarly multi-pronged (see also Dawson, 2021; Rundle et al., 2020). By analogy, reducing serious traffic accidents involves understanding why serious traffic accidents happen and intervening on the most powerful contributing factors: Is it bad brakes, bad airbags, bad roads, high speed limits, or bad driver education? To reduce cheating, interventions may target the many factors that influence perceptions, evaluations, and decisions.

Because many cases of cheating are unintentional and explicit discussions of cheating are rare, strengthening academic integrity education would likely be impactful (Blum, 2009; Brown & Janssen, 2017; Curtis et al., 2013). Educators can strengthen students' perceptions of cheating by providing consistent, standardized, and concrete guidelines on what students are allowed to do and, conversely, what they are not allowed to do. And because students sometimes evaluate cheating as okay in certain circumstances as when facing high pressures, educators may adjust the nature or framing of assignments to reduce the likelihood of these circumstances. At the decision step, to prevent students from believing that they have no choice but to cheat, educators can provide resources to navigate time management or split large assignments into several smaller assignments with lower stakes (e.g., Lang, 2013; Lederman, 2021).

In this chapter, we refrained from defining cheating as immoral. In the same vein, we refrain from insisting that educators must necessarily adopt every strategy that might reduce cheating. Educators, like students, balance multiple concerns in their academic lives. Academic integrity is one major concern but so is time-management, academic rigor, and validity of assessments. As academic integrity researchers, we see our role as that of advancing the scientific knowledge of why students cheat and, ultimately, how educators and institutions may promote academic integrity and reduce cheating. Insofar as such knowledge helps students, educators, educational institutions, and our broader society—as we believe it will—the science of academic integrity will continue to play a key role in the coming decades.

REFERENCES

Ajzen, I. and Fishbein, M. (2005). 'The influence of attitudes on behavior'. In D. Albarracín, B. T. Johnson and M. P. Zanna (Eds), *The handbook of attitudes* (pp. 173–221). Lawrence Erlbaum Associates Publishers.

Anderman, E. M. and Midgley, C. (2004). 'Changes in self-reported academic cheating across the transition from middle school to high school', *Contemporary Educational Psychology, 29*, pp. 499–517.

Ariely, D. (2012). *The honest truth about dishonesty: How we lie to everyone—especially ourselves.* New York: Harper Collins.

Ashworth, P., Bannister, P. and Thorne, P. (1997). 'Guilty in whose eyes? University students' perceptions of cheating and plagiarism in academic work and assessment', *Studies in Higher Education, 22*(2), pp. 187–203.

Ashworth, P., Freewood, M. and Macdonald, R. (2003). 'The student lifeworld and the meanings of plagiarism', *Journal of Phenomenological Psychology, 34*, pp. 257–278.

Baird, J. S. (1980). 'Current trends in college cheating', *Psychology in the Schools, 17*(4), pp. 515–522.

Bandura, A. (2016). *Moral disengagement: How people do harm and live with themselves.* New York: Macmillan Higher Education.

Bareket-Shavit, C., Baxley, C., Chen, K., Waltzer, T. and Dahl, A. (2018). 'Do teachers teach students what they need to learn about academic misconduct?', *Poster at the Annual Meeting of the Association for Psychological Science,* San Francisco, CA.

Barnhardt, B. (2016). 'The "epidemic" of cheating depends on its definition: A critique of inferring the moral quality of "cheating in any form"', *Ethics & Behavior, 26*(4), pp. 330–343.

Beasley, E. M. (2016). 'Comparing the demographics of students reported for academic dishonesty to those of the overall student population', *Ethics & Behavior, 26*(1), pp. 45–62.

Bertram Gallant, T. (Ed.). (2011). *Creating the ethical academy: A systems approach to understanding misconduct and empowering change.* Routledge.

Bertram Gallant, T., Binkin, N. and Donohue, M. (2015). 'Students at risk for being reported for cheating', *Journal of Academic Ethics, 13,* pp. 217–228.

Bertram Gallant, T. and Stephens, J. M. (2020). 'Punishment is not enough: The moral imperative of responding to cheating with a developmental approach', *Journal of College & Character, 21,* pp. 57–66.

Bidgood, J. and Merrill, J. B. (2017). 'As computer coding classes swell, so does cheating'. *New York Times,* May 29. Retrieved from: **https://www.nytimes.com/2017/05/29/us/computer-science-cheating.html** (Accessed Septembner 20, 2021).

Blasi, A. (1980). 'Bridging moral cognition and moral action: A critical review of the literature', *Psychological Bulletin, 88*(1), pp. 1–45.

Blum, S. D. (2009). 'Academic integrity and student plagiarism: A question of education, not ethics', *The Chronicle of Higher Education, 55*(24), p. A35.

Borg, E. (2009). 'Local plagiarisms', *Assessment & Evaluation in Higher Education, 34,* pp. 415–426.

Bretag, T. (Ed.) (2020). *A research agenda for academic integrity.* Edward Elgar Publishing.

Brown, D. L. (2002). 'Cheating must be okay—everybody does it!', *Nurse Educator, 27*(1), pp. 6–8.

Brown, N. and Janssen, R. (2017). 'Preventing plagiarism and fostering academic integrity: A practical approach', *Journal of Perspectives in Applied Academic Practice, 5*(3), pp. 102–109.

Bunn, D., Caudill, S. and Gropper, D. (1992). 'Crime in the classroom: An economic analysis of undergraduate student cheating behavior', *The Journal of Economic Education, 23*, pp. 197–207.

Chace, W. M. (2012). 'A question of honor', *The American Scholar, 81*(2), pp. 20–32.

Childers, D. R. and Bruton, S. (2016). '"Should it be considered plagiarism?" Student perceptions of complex citation issues', *Journal of Academic Ethics, 14*, pp. 1–17.

Chou, I. (2010). 'Is plagiarism a culture product: The voice of a Chinese-speaking ELL student', *The International Journal—Language, Society and Culture, 31*, pp. 37–41.

Cizek, G. J. (2003). *Detecting and preventing classroom cheating: Promoting integrity in assessment.* Dallas, TX: Corwin Press.

Curtis, G. J., Gouldthorp, B., Thomas, E. F., O'Brien, G. M. and Correia, H. M. (2013). 'Online academic-integrity mastery training may improve students' awareness of, and attitudes toward, plagiarism', *Psychology Learning & Teaching, 12*(3), pp. 282–289.

Curtis, G. J. and Vardanega, L. (2016). 'Is plagiarism changing over time? A 10-year time-lag study with three points of measurement', *Higher Education Research & Development, 35*, pp. 1167–1179.

Dahl, A., Gingo, M., Uttich, K. and Turiel, E. (2018). 'Moral reasoning about human welfare in adolescents and adults: Judging conflicts involving sacrificing and saving lives', *Monographs of the Society for Research in Child Development, Serial No. 330, 83*(3), pp. 1–109.

Dahl, A. and Waltzer, T. (2018). 'Moral disengagement as a psychological construct', *American Journal of Psychology, 131*, pp. 240–246.

Dahl, A. and Waltzer, T. (2020). 'Rationalization is rare, reasoning is pervasive', *Behavioral and Brain Sciences, 43*, p. e75.

Davis, S. F., Grover, C. A., Becker, A. H. and McGregor, L. N. (1992). 'Academic dishonesty: Prevalence, determinants, techniques, and punishments', *Teaching of Psychology, 19*, pp. 16–20.

Dawson, P. (2021). 'Surveillance, cheating and academic integrity: What can we leave behind?' *Talk presented at the UC Davis Symposium on Assessment of Learning,* Virtual.

DeBernardi, F. C., Waltzer, T. and Dahl, A. (2021). Cheating contextualized: How academic pressures lead to moral exceptions. *Talk presented at the 47th Annual Association for Moral Education Conference,* Virtual.

DePaulo, B. M., Kashy, D. A., Kirkendol, S. E., Wyer, M. M. and Epstein, J. A. (1996). 'Lying in everyday life', *Journal of Personality and Social Psychology, 70*(5), pp. 979–995.

Drake, C. A. (1941). 'Why students cheat', *Journal of Higher Education, 12,* pp. 418–420.

Fiske, A. P. and Rai, T. S. (2014). *Virtuous violence: Hurting and killing to create, sustain, end, and honor social relationships.* Cambridge University Press.

Freeman, V. G., Rathore, S. S., Weinfurt, K. P., Schulman, K. A. and Sulmasy, D. P. (1999). 'Lying for patients: Physician deception of third-party payers', *Archives of Internal Medicine, 159*(19), pp. 2263–2270.

Galloway, M. K. (2012). 'Cheating in advantaged high schools: Prevalence, justifications, and possibilities for change', *Ethics & Behavior, 22*(5), pp. 378–399.

Gert, B. (2004). *Common morality: Deciding what to do.* Oxford: Oxford University Press.

Giluk, T. L. and Postlethwaite, B. E. (2015). 'Big five personality and academic dishonesty: A meta-analytic review', *Personality and Individual Differences, 72,* pp. 59–67.

Gingo, M. (2017). 'Children's reasoning about deception and defiance as ways of resisting parents' and teachers' directives', *Developmental Psychology, 53*(9), pp. 1643–1655.

Green, S. P. (2006). *Lying, cheating, and stealing: A moral theory of white-collar crime*. New York: Oxford University Press.

Gullifer, J and Tyson, G. (2014). 'Who has read the policy on plagiarism? Unpacking students' understanding of plagiarism', *Studies in Higher Education, 39*, pp. 1202–1218.

Haines, V. J., Diekhoff, G. M., LaBeff, E. E. and Clark, R. E. (1986). 'College cheating: Immaturity, lack of commitment, and the neutralizing attitude', *Research in Higher Education, 25*(4), pp. 342–354.

Hallborg, R. (1997). 'Comparing harms: The lesser-evil defense and the trolley problem', *Legal Theory, 3*(4), pp. 291–316.

Hartshorne, H. and May, M. A. (1928). *Studies in the nature of character: Vol. I. Studies in deceit*. New York: Macmillan.

Hayes, N. and Introna, L. D. (2005). 'Cultural values, plagiarism, and fairness: When plagiarism gets in the way of learning', *Ethics & Behavior, 15*, pp. 213–231.

Hodgkinson, T., Curtis, H., MacAlister, D. and Farrell, G. (2016). 'Student academic dishonesty: The potential for situational prevention', *Journal of Criminal Justice Education, 27*(1), pp. 1–18.

Houston, J. P. (1976). 'Amount and loci of classroom answer copying, spaced seating, and alternate test forms', *Journal of Educational Psychology, 68*, pp. 729–735.

Husain, F. M., Al-Shaibani, G. K. S. and Mahfoodh, O. H. A. (2017). 'Perceptions of and attitudes toward plagiarism and factors contributing to plagiarism: A review of studies', *Journal of Academic Ethics, 15*(2), pp. 167–195.

Jambon, M. and Smetana, J. G. (2014). 'Moral complexity in middle childhood: Children's evaluations of necessary harm', *Developmental Psychology, 50*(1), pp. 22–33.

Jensen, L. A., Arnett, J. J., Feldman, S. S. and Cauffman, E. (2002). 'It's wrong, but everybody does it: Academic dishonesty among high school and college students', *Contemporary Educational Psychology, 27*(2), pp. 209–228.

Jensen, L. A., Arnett, J. J., Feldman, S. S. and Cauffman, E. (2004). 'The right to do wrong: Lying to parents among adolescents and emerging adults', *Journal of Youth and Adolescence, 33*(2), pp. 101–112.

Jordan, A. E. (2001). 'College student cheating: The role of motivation, perceived norms, attitudes, and knowledge of institutional policy', *Ethics & Behavior 11*(3), pp. 233–247.

Karlins, M., Michaels, C. and Podlogar, S. (1988). 'An empirical investigation of actual cheating in a large sample of undergraduates', *Research in Higher Education, 29*(4), pp. 359–364.

Killen, M. and Dahl, A. (2021). 'Moral reasoning enables developmental and societal change', *Perspectives on Psychological Science, 16*(6), pp. 1209–1225..

Kohlberg, L. (1971). 'From is to ought: How to commit the naturalistic fallacy and get away with it in the study of moral development'. In T. Mischel (Ed.), *Cognitive development and epistemology* (pp. 151–235). New York: Academic Press.

Lang, J. M. (2013). *Cheating lessons: Learning from academic dishonesty.* Cambridge, MA: Harvard University Press.

Lederman, D. (2021). 'Combating cheating in the COVID era', *Inside Higher Ed.*, February 17. Retrieved from: **https://www. insidehighered.com/quicktakes/2021/02/17/combating-cheating-covid-era-key-podcast** (Accessed September 20, 2021).

Lee, J. A., Bardi, A., Gerrans, P., Sneddon, J., van Herk, H., Evers, U. and Schwartz, S. (2021). 'Are value–behavior relations stronger than previously thought? It depends on value importance', *European Journal of Personality.*

Lee, S. D., Kuncel, N. R. and Gau, J. (2020). 'Personality, attitude, and demographic correlates of academic dishonesty: A meta-analysis', *Psychological Bulletin, 146*(11), pp. 1042–1058.

Levine, T. R., Kim, R. K., and Hamel, L. M. (2010). 'People lie for a reason: Three experiments documenting the principle of veracity', *Communication Research Reports, 27*(4), pp. 271–285.

McCabe, D. L. (1997). 'Classroom cheating among natural science and engineering majors', *Science and Engineering Ethics, 3*, pp. 433–445.

McCabe, D. L., Butterfield, K. D. and Treviño, L. K. (2012). *Cheating in college: Why students do it and what educators can do about it*. Baltimore, MD: Johns Hopkins Press.

McCabe, D. L. and Treviño, L. K. (1995). 'Cheating among business students: A challenge for business leaders and educators', *Journal of Management Education, 19*(2), pp. 205–218.

McCabe, D. L., Treviño, L. K. and Butterfield, K. D. (2001). 'Cheating in academic institutions: A decade of research', *Ethics & Behavior, 11*(3), pp. 219–232.

McLeod, A. and Simkin, M. G. (2010). 'Why do college students cheat?', *Journal of Business Ethics, 94,* pp. 441–453.

Miller, A. D., Murdock, T. B., Anderman, E. M. and Poindexter, A. L. (2007). 'Who are all these cheaters? Characteristics of academically dishonest students'. In E. M. Anderman and T. B. Murdock (Eds), *Psychology of academic cheating* (pp. 9–32). Burlington, MA: Elsevier Academic Press.

Miller, A., Shoptaugh, C. and Wooldridge, J. (2011). 'Reasons not to cheat, academic-integrity responsibility, and frequency of cheating', *The Journal of Experimental Education, 79,* pp. 169–184.

Modi, R., Waltzer, T., & Dahl, A. (2021). 'Why do so many students cheat in engineering? Perceptions, evaluations, and justifications'. *Poster presented at the Society for Research in Child Development biennial meeting,* Virtual.

Murdock, T. B., Miller, A. D. and Kohlhardt, J. (2004). 'Effects of classroom context variables on high school students' judgments of the acceptability and likelihood of cheating', *Journal of Educational Psychology, 96*(4), pp. 765–777.

Murdock, T. B., Stephens, J. M. and Grotewiel, M. M. (2016). 'Student dishonesty in the face of assessment: Who, why, and what we can do about it'. In G. T. Brown and L. Harris (Eds), *Handbook of human factors and social conditions in assessment* (pp. 186–203). London: Routledge.

Nucci, L. P., Turiel, E. and Roded, A. D. (2017). 'Continuities and discontinuities in the development of moral judgments', *Human Development, 60,* pp. 279–341.

Ogilvie, J. and Stewart, A. (2010). 'The integration of rational choice and self-efficacy theories: A situational analysis of student misconduct', *Australian and New Zealand Journal of Criminology, 43*(1), pp. 130–155.

Olafson, L., Schraw, G. and Kehrwald, N. (2014). 'Academic dishonesty: Behaviors, sanctions, and retention of adjudicated college students', *Journal of College Student Development, 55,* pp. 661–674.

Olson, K. R. and Shaw, A. (2010). '"No fair, copycat!": What children's response to plagiarism tells us about their understanding of ideas', *Developmental Science, 14,* pp. 431–439.

Park, C. (2003). 'In other (people's) words: Plagiarism by university students—literature and lessons', *Assessment and Evaluation in Higher Education, 28,* pp. 471–488.

Perkins, S. A. and Turiel, E. (2007). 'To lie or not to lie: To whom and under what circumstances', *Child Development, 78*(2), pp. 609–621.

Pennycook, A. (1996). 'Borrowing others' words: Text, ownership, memory, and plagiarism', *TESOL Quarterly, 30,* pp. 201–230.

Power, L. G. (2009). 'University students' perceptions of plagiarism', *The Journal of Higher Education, 80,* pp. 643–662.

Rettinger, D. A. (2007). 'Applying decision theory to academic integrity decisions'. In T. B. Murdock and E. M. Anderman (Eds), *Psychology of academic cheating* (pp. 141–167). Burlington, MA: Elsevier Academic Press.

Rettinger, D. A. (2017). 'The role of emotions and attitudes in causing and preventing cheating', *Theory Into Practice, 56*(2), pp. 103–110.

Rettinger, D. A. and Jordan, A. E. (2005). 'The relations among religion, motivation, and college cheating: A natural experiment', *Ethics & Behavior, 15*(2), pp. 107–129.

Rettinger, D. A. and Kramer, Y. (2009). 'Situational and personal causes of student cheating', *Research in Higher Education, 50*(3), pp. 293–313.

Roig, M. (1997). 'Can undergraduate students determine whether text has been plagiarized?', *Psychological Record, 47*, pp. 113–122.

Roig, M. (2001). 'Plagiarism and paraphrasing criteria of college and university professors', *Ethics & Behavior, 11*, pp. 307–323.

Rundle, K., Curtis, G. J. and Clare, J. (2019). 'Why students do not engage in contract cheating', *Frontiers in Psychology, 10*, p. 2229.

Rundle, K., Curtis, G. J. and Clare, J. (2020). 'Why students choose not to cheat'. In T. Bretag (Ed.), *A research agenda for academic integrity* (pp. 100–111). Elgar Research Agendas.

Russell, J. (2014). 'Is there a normatively distinctive concept of cheating in sport (or anywhere else)?', *Journal of the Philosophy of Sport, 41*(3), pp. 303–323.

Samuelson, A., Waltzer, T. and Dahl, A. (2021). 'First- and third-person moral evaluations about real cases of cheating', *Poster presented at the 47th Annual Association for Moral Education Conference,* Virtual.

Serota, K. B., Levine, T. R. and Boster, F. J. (2010). 'The prevalence of lying in America: Three studies of self-reported lies', *Human Communication Research, 36*(1), pp. 2–25.

Stephens, J. M. (2018). 'Bridging the divide: The role of motivation and self-regulation in explaining the judgment-action gap related to academic dishonesty', *Frontiers in Psychology, 9*.

Stephens, J. M. and Nicholson, H. (2008). 'Cases of incongruity: Exploring the divide between adolescents' beliefs and behaviors related to academic cheating', *Educational Studies, 34*, pp. 361–376.

Sun, X. and Hu, G. (2020). 'What do academics know and do about plagiarism? An interview study with Chinese university teachers of English', *Ethics & Behavior, 30*(6), pp. 459–479.

Sykes, G. M. and Matza, D. (1957). 'Techniques of neutralization: A theory of delinquency', *American Sociological Review, 22*, pp. 664–670.

Teixeira, A. A. C. and Rocha, M. F. (2010). 'Cheating by economics and business undergraduate students: An exploratory international assessment', *Higher Education, 59*, pp. 663–701.

Turiel, E. (2003). 'Morals, motives and actions', *British Journal of Developmental Psychology Monograph Series, 2,* pp. 29–40.

Turiel, E. and Dahl, A. (2019). 'The development of domains of moral and conventional norms, coordination in decision-making, and the implications of social opposition'. In K. Bayertz and N. Boughley (Eds), *The normative animal: On the biological significance of social, moral, and linguistic norms.* Oxford University Press.

Wainryb, C. (1991). 'Understanding differences in moral judgments: The role of informational assumptions', *Child Development, 62,* pp. 840–851.

Wainryb, C., Shaw, L. A., Langley, M., Cottam, K. and Lewis, R. (2004). 'Children's thinking about diversity of belief in the early school years: Judgments of relativism, tolerance, and disagreeing persons', *Child Development, 75*(3), pp. 687–703.

Waltzer, T., Baxley, C., Bareket-Shavit, C. and Dahl, A. (2018). 'Reasoning and decision-making behind plagiarism'. *Paper presented at the Annual Meeting of the Association for Psychological Science,* San Francisco, CA.

Waltzer, T. and Dahl, A. (2021). 'Students' perceptions and evaluations of plagiarism: Effects of text and context', *Journal of Moral Education, 50*(4), pp. 436–451.

Waltzer, T., Dahl, A., Samuelson, A., Chen, K., Baxley, C. and Bareket-Shavit, C. (2019). 'Narrowing the judgment-action gap: The case of student cheating', *Poster presented at the Society for Philosophy and Psychology annual meeting,* San Diego, CA.

Waltzer, T., Samuelson, A. and Dahl, A. (2021). 'Students' reasoning about whether to report when others cheat: Conflict, confusion, and consequences', *Journal of Academic Ethics.*

Waytz, A., Dungan, J. and Young, L. (2013). 'The whistleblower's dilemma and the fairness–loyalty tradeoff', *Journal of Experimental Social Psychology, 49*(6), pp. 1027–1033.

Whitley, B. E. (1998). 'Factors associated with cheating among college students: A review', *Research in Higher Education, 39*, pp. 235–274.

Zhao, L., Heyman, G. D., Chen, L., Sun, W., Zhang, R. and Lee, K. (2019). 'Cheating in the name of others: Offering prosocial justifications promotes unethical behavior in young children', *Journal of Experimental Child Psychology, 177,* pp. 187–196.

Zhao, L., Zheng, J., Mao, H., Yu, X., Ye, J., Chen, H., Compton, B. J., Heyman, G. D. and Lee, K. (2021). 'Effects of trust and threat messaging on academic cheating: A field study', *Psychological Science, 32*(5), pp. 735–742.

CHAPTER 6

It's in the Pedagogy: Evidence-Based Practices to Promote Academic Integrity

Jacqueline A. Goldman[1], Mariko L. Carson[2] and Jennifer Simonds[3]

[1]School of Psychological Science, Oregon State University

[2]School of Business, Howard University

[3]Office of Academic Integrity & Accountability, University of Maryland Global Campus

Plagiarism and other forms of academic misconduct have historically been conceptualized as the intentional and rational decision to cheat (Bertram Gallant, 2008). This conceptualization is reflected in the legalistic language often used to portray academic misconduct and the students who engage in academically prohibited behaviors (Diamond, 2019), and in the ways institutions address academic misconduct (Merkel, 2021). However, these assumptions neglect the underlying environmental and individual factors that can lead to reports of academic integrity violations.

Examination of historic instructional practices and how they privilege some and marginalize others is crucial to equitable academic integrity management. Inequity rooted in the elitist privileges, and biases that form academic standards and expectations are rarely challenged (McGee, 2020). As a result, the contributing factors that drive students to engage in academic misconduct are enhanced for those from underrepresented and marginalized backgrounds (Strangfeld, 2019). These inequities (Carter, 2018) form the basis for policies and resulting decisions. In approaching such concerns with biases and inequities in mind, educators can begin to understand the argument for reimagining pedagogy that both supports success for all students and that can, in turn, decrease academic misconduct. Any effort to promote meaningful academic integrity requires a holistic mindset with attention to and action on equity issues as well as a shift in philosophy from a mindset focused on deficits to one based on growth (i.e. growth mindset) (e.g. Miles, 2018).

In this paper, we identify factors in the external environment and characteristics of individual students that can contribute to academic misconduct. From this basis, we outline pedagogical practices that directly address factors that can lead students into unauthorized actions. Finally, we present examples of High Impact Practices (HIPs) that serve as frameworks through which pedagogical strategies can be utilized to alleviate potential barriers to learning and support students in their efforts to complete work with integrity.

FACTORS INFLUENCING STUDENT ENGAGEMENT IN ACADEMIC MISCONDUCT

Many of the reasons for academic misconduct can be found in the external environment. These influences can include online resourcing, course quality variables, instructor engagement practices, and pedagogy that emphasizes performance over mastery. Students increasingly navigate online materials that present temptation and opportunity to engage in academic misconduct (Greenberger et al., 2016). Temptation is exacerbated by highly manipulative language that contract cheating companies use to engage students in their services (Crook and Nixon, 2020). Perceptions of poor course quality or inadequate instruction may be rationalizations for academic misconduct (Rettinger and Kramer, 2009) or genuine obstacles that lead to desperate choices (Devlin and Gray, 2007), especially when instructors are disengaged or courses are disorganized (Anderman and Murdock, 2007). Also, course designs that emphasize performance over mastery can increase external pressure on student achievement and put students at risk of academic misconduct (Corrion et al., 2010). Student perceptions that academic integrity is not important or that their peers are engaging in misconduct are reliable predictors of students' own academic misconduct (McCabe et al., 2001).

Individual factors that have shown relationships to engagement in academic misconduct include issues related to time management (McCabe et al., 1999), stress and pressure (Schmelkin et al., 2008), skill gaps (Amigud and Lancaster, 2019), and extrinsic motivation (Murdock and Anderman, 2006; Rettinger and Kramer, 2009). Cultural differences may result in behaviors that are considered academic misconduct in, for instance, Western institutions but not in Asian institutions that prioritize memorization and verbatim repetition (Hayes and Introna, 2005). Collectively, these influences on academic misconduct lead to complex interpretations of students' choices when compounded with resource, educational, and positional inequities that students may be experiencing.

Inequities in education (Carter, 2018) influence the development and implementation of policies. When students' identities and experiences are not considered and when they face biased and microaggressive treatment, two forms of inequity frequently occur in tandem (Carter, 2007). There is a risk of academic trauma which can lead to students feeling disconnected and discouraged and can impact their persistence in their studies, potentially leading to academic attrition (Franklin et al., 2006). Strangfeld (2019) examined student explanations for instances of plagiarism and concluded that many of the reasons provided were rooted in "historical impacts of systemic inequities and cultural capital" (p. 11). In qualitative interviews, students cited fears of not sounding "like a college student" primarily due to their differences in linguistic style and "writtenness". These student fears and teacher expectations based on assumed cultural capital, and familiarity with prevailing societal norms (Bourdieu, 1977 as cited in Strangfeld, 2019) can result in students being penalized for not possessing certain knowledge.

Similarly, standards that do not embrace linguistic diversity can lead students to infer that their authentic voices are devalued and unwelcome (Hudley et al., 2020), especially when grading mechanisms castigate rather than honor authenticity. Narrow standards can pose challenges because instructors want students to communicate in ways that the primary audience (usually the instructor) understands, but also limits what are considered acceptable deviations from the practice of allowing students to be original in their thought and delivery. Using biased grading systems (e.g. Spinelli, 2008), though, can impact student self-efficacy, a student's confidence in their own abilities to succeed in a task (Bandura, 1997), and result in students providing what they believe the instructor would prefer to see rather than what the student can deliver. This can lead to seeking out unauthorized means to complete coursework.

In addition, biased teaching and perspectives along with the authoritative privilege of instructors has the potential to cultivate a deficit mindset, the focus on what students *lack* in terms of resources, skills, and knowledge that are necessary to be successful within the dominant higher education environment. Approaches to diversity in education typically use a deficit framework to conceptualize the needs of students who are from backgrounds underrepresented in higher education (Smit, 2007), and multicultural educational efforts have tended to focus on what students *cannot* do (Gay, 2018). Gershenson and Papageorge (2018) showed that college completion rates were higher for students whose teachers rated their expectations of student achievement higher. Specifically, White teachers showed significantly lower expectations for Black students than for "similarly situated" White students. Students who display signs of lower achievement, frequently due to environmental realities of underrepresented backgrounds, are also at risk of generalized negative faculty perceptions (e.g. Rubie-Davies, 2010). When applied to academic misconduct, a deficit mindset creates a bias that can easily justify punitive responses because students from underrepresented backgrounds are viewed as needing correction.

PEDAGOGICAL SOLUTIONS FOR PROMOTING INTEGRITY

Students, especially students from groups such as first-generation college students, rarely engage in academic misconduct because of malice (Devlin and Gray, 2007). Whether those rationales are based on personal or environmental factors, engaging in academic misconduct can be prevented or lessened by adapting more compassionate, clear, and structured pedagogy. Moving from deficit thinking to the view that educators can facilitate learning and remove barriers through pedagogical strategies can assist students in relying less on unauthorized academic shortcuts. Environmental and personal perspectives and the negatives affiliated with inequity will continue to be our contexts to frame pedagogical recommendations for alleviating these temptations. Table 1 provides a summary connecting reasons for academic misconduct to strategies that can address them.

UTILITY AND RELEVANCE OF ASSIGNMENTS

When considering external factors that may entice a student to engage in academic misconduct, a major theme is a lack of caring about the curriculum/course (Hattingh et al., 2020). Why should students exert effort if the material or assignment is not personally relevant or does not benefit them directly? While not every course and lesson will be personally meaningful to each student, educators can still create assignments that demonstrate utility or usefulness to students. Specifically, when designing course content, both instruction and assessments, providing clear utility and relevance increases student interest in course material and increases performance (Hulleman et al., 2017).

136

Table 1   Summary of Pedagogical Strategies and High Impact Practices (HIPs) to Address Reasons for Academic Misconduct

Reasons for Engagement in Academic Misconduct	General Pedagogy Strategies	HIP-Informed Strategies
Temptation & Opportunity	Provide unique assignments that disallow use of search engine answers as well as clear expectations for what the assignment expectations are so the student does not need to seek out external tools for clarification.	Design projects that are customized and specific.
Other Students Engaging in Misconduct	Provide personal relevance and utility in assignment creation so students find the merit in the course to their personal goals.	Create a structure for students to share and/or collaborate on projects so that one's original work is transparent to others.
Course/Instructor Problems	Design courses to be clear in expectations and provide utility or discussion of relevance of assignments and learning outcomes.	Shift from instructor as giver of knowledge to facilitator. Promote high engagement and relevance through project framework.
Perception that Academic Integrity is Not Important	Provide clear discourse and examples as to how to properly avoid academic misconduct and rationale as to why the assignments are important (provide utility)	Create community expectations through the role of facilitator and integrate integrity statements about creating original work.

(Continued)

137

Table 1 (Continued)

Reasons for Engagement in Academic Misconduct	General Pedagogy Strategies	HIP-Informed Strategies
Lack of Clarity About What is Allowed	Provide clear discourse and examples as to how to properly avoid academic misconduct and rationale as to why the assignments are important (provide utility)	Design project instructions to convey expectations for original work and delineate where information from attributed sources is needed and appropriate.
Priority on Performance over Mastery	Break up large assignments into smaller components to remove the performative and daunting grade component of large assignments. Give ample opportunities for students to build self-efficacy.	Use the inherently iterative nature of project progression to emphasize process over or alongside product.
Cultural Capital Issues	Culturally Responsive Teaching brings student culture in as a course element.	Engage support skills that integrate with content learning, especially in service-learning, through project design.
Time Management Skills; Perseverance; Self-Control	Break up large assignments into smaller components to force students to engage in time management, also allowing for ample opportunities to provide critical feedback and catch errant behavior early on.	Use the structure of project steps to create milestone deadlines. Motivate students through subsequent steps being dependent on success on previous steps.

(Continued)

138

Table 1   (Continued)

Reasons for Engagement in Academic Misconduct	General Pedagogy Strategies	HIP-Informed Strategies
Skill Gaps	Provide ample and explicit feedback on assignments to help demonstrate key skills and knowledge that students may need to work on to help bridge skill gaps and foster self-efficacy	Provide opportunities to increase student confidence through mastery of project steps and enhance content knowledge through designing application of knowledge in the project.
Stress & Pressure	Demonstrate clear utility and relatedness within the course structure, allowing students to feel comfortable to lean into stress and feel as though they can reach out within the learning partnership.	Facilitate intrinsic motivation decrease in traditional academic assessment formats and increase in student abilities through project steps.
Extrinsic Motivation	Provide clear utility value and relatedness within the course structure and assignments, demonstrating an intrinsic value for students to complete the course and assignments.	In service-learning particularly, draw explicit community context connections to goals outside of one's own external motivators
International Student Background	Provide clear instructions that convey what is expected and set academic integrity standards with learning resources available.	Make the need for students to develop and share original ideas and arguments in project instructions.

Student choice and engagement in a task is heavily influenced by expectancy beliefs for success and subjective task values (Eccles, 1983). According to Expectancy Value Theory (EVT), student effort and engagement are influenced by a student's own confidence in their success at the task (expectancy beliefs) as well as how much they perceive the task to be important to their self-identity (attainment value), enjoyable (intrinsic value), personally useful (utility value), and low in personal or resource cost (cost value). While expectancy beliefs can be related to self-efficacy and have bearing on student choice, subjective task values are related to intrinsic motivation, interest, and task persistence, which are important characteristics that may lead to engagement (or not) in academic misconduct.

Research conducted on EVT and subjective task values has found that fostering individual interest via perceptions of value can enhance student motivation and personal utility (Hulleman and Harackiewicz, 2009; Hulleman et al., 2010, 2017). Given that students who cheat may do so due to low personal or professional relevance, increasing personal utility may help to alleviate cheating behavior. Increasing utility can occur through various pedagogical methods. Hulleman and Harackiewicz (2009) and Hulleman et al. (2010) found that high school and college students who wrote about the relevance of course content to their lives demonstrated not only an increase in utility value but found greater interest in course material and higher course grades. These findings were also more prominent for students who had lower competence in course content, perceived (performance expectations) or actual (previous performance on course assignments). Facilitating a connection to course material that provides relevance and increased perception of importance for students is, therefore, one method to help alleviate academic misconduct (Schraw et al., 2007).

Instructors should promote the utility and relevance of assignments (Hulleman, et al., 2010) as a means of helping students make connections between academic and non-academic life. This practice is in line with the principles of Culturally Relevant Teaching (CRT). Gay (2018). . .

CLARITY OF EXPECTATIONS

Not only does fair pedagogy give explicit expectations that can reduce cheating behavior (MacGregor and Stuebs, 2012), but clarity in pedagogy can also impact the likelihood of engaging in academic misconduct. For some students, engaging in academic misconduct may be the result of perceived ambiguity about whether the behavior is allowable due to uncertain or disorganized course structure (MacGregor and Stuebs, 2012). Guibert and Michauet (2011) found that at least 85 percent of students reported to have not read the university standards regarding academic misconduct despite inclusion of the standards in student orientations and within syllabi. Expecting students to inherently understand academic misconduct policy is a problematic assumption that can further the inequity experienced by students unfamiliar with higher education culture. To counteract this obstacle, providing clear learning goals, outcomes, and explicit description of what constitutes academic misconduct within that course can be a major step in eliminating academic misconduct (Ambrose et al., 2010). Within writing assignments, for example, explicit directions for referencing material can help clarify expectations (McCabe and Pavela, 2004). Many students who plagiarize may be unaware that their behavior was

141

problematic or explicitly against the course standards (Beasley, 2014). Inconsistencies and disagreements about what is considered academic misconduct have been found among students (Jensen et al., 2002) and among faculty themselves (Bennett et al., 2011). Merkel (2021) showed that plagiarism policies and practices differed widely even within one institution.

By demonstrating appropriate ways to cite, reference, and summarize through course materials that include definitions and examples, students can develop a clearer understanding of expectations and avoid inadvertent academic misconduct. Instructor-led demonstrations in class can also provide clear guidance on academic integrity. While instructor guidance is important, students may encounter differences across classes. Therefore, the responsibility for academic integrity education should not be placed solely on instructors. Faculty, staff, and administrators all share responsibility in academic integrity matters (Garza Mitchell and Parnther, 2018). Institutions can adopt a unified collaborative approach to academic integrity by establishing an institutional definition of academic integrity, communicating expectations through tutorials and advising sessions, and reiterating these expectations in the classroom.

LEARNING PARTNERSHIPS

Previous research has indicated that students may also be motivated to engage in cheating behavior because they feel as if the instructor does not care about them as students (MacGregor and Stuebs, 2012). With increasing course sizes and external demands on educators, facilitating an authentic relationship with students may feel impractical or nearly impossible. While regular and meaningful one-on-one interaction with students may not be possible, pedagogical practices can facilitate relatedness and a sense of community within the classroom itself. Deci and Ryan's Self-Determination mini-theory (2000) argues that to facilitate general wellness, integrity, and internalization of course values, humans have three basic needs that must be fulfilled: autonomy, competence, and relatedness (Deci and Ryan, 2017). Although fulfilling all three needs has benefits for motivation and learning in the classroom (Deci and Ryan, 2000), the fulfillment of just the relatedness need has unique benefits, such as fostering a sense of community within a classroom setting. When the need for relatedness is met, students tend to internalize and accept values as their own (Niemiec and Ryan, 2009).

Further, research on the importance of relatedness and connection in the classroom is corroborated in discussions on learning partnerships. Brookfield discusses the importance of authentic connection between educators and students in *The Skillful Teacher* (2000):

Not trusting teachers has several consequences for students. They are unwilling to submit themselves to the perilous uncertainties of new learning. They avoid risk. They keep their most deeply felt concerns private. They view with cynical reserve the exhortations and instructions of teachers. (p. 162)

To fulfill student needs for relatedness, as well as foster a sense of trustworthiness, educators should create what Hammond (2016) calls learning partnerships, relationships based on affirmation, mutual respect, and validation. Within a learning partnership, students are affirmed by the educator acknowledging that they have unique culturally specific traits. Educators can allow students to represent their authentic selves by providing assignments and opportunities to express their distinctive backgrounds and identities within a safe space. These opportunities to express personal experiences allow students to feel an authentic connection to classmates and the instructor (Magolda and King, 2004). Facilitating these connections within the classroom setting allows relatedness needs to be fulfilled, leading to internalization of course values and practices (Niemic and Ryan, 2009). Fulfilling these needs also creates an authentic connection, which can lead to students being less likely to engage in academic misconduct when they feel valued by their instructor (Beasley, 2014; MacGregor and Stuebs, 2012). Educators can provide opportunities for self-expression by allowing students to choose writing topics and prompts (Deci and Ryan, 2015), providing assignments that require students to connect material to their everyday experience (Heddy and Sinatra, 2013), and providing discussion prompts that allow students to reflect and share their own culture and background (DeNoyelles et al., 2014). These practices can foster learning partnerships, increase student relatedness, and lower the likelihood of academic misconduct.

LOW STAKES ASSESSMENTS WITH FEEDBACK

Although many factors that influence cheating behavior may be beyond the influence of the educator (e.g. peer behavior, ease of access to materials) educators can address personal factors through evidence-based pedagogical practices that can curtail the allure of engaging in academic misconduct. One major rationale that students provide for academic misconduct is procrastination due to poor time management (Crook and Nixon, 2021; Schmelkin et al., 2008). Some pedagogical structures can be implemented within the course and assignment design to encourage time management.

One option is to break up major assignments or papers into smaller components throughout the semester (Sterngold, 2004) so students are required to work on the project over time instead of waiting until the last minute (Beasley 2014). Having students turn in multiple "steps" of the assignment also gives instructors multiple opportunities to catch mistakes (misconduct or otherwise) and to provide formative feedback to for the completed project. This process also can alleviate the enticement of taking unauthorized shortcuts from feeling the course or assignment is too disorganized (McCabe and Pavela, 2004).

Further personal factors that may be alleviated through course design are a lack of confidence and perceived incompetence to complete course work (McCabe et al., 2001). Students have distinctly different educational backgrounds and preparedness due to educational inequities, but even students who are well prepared may find themselves struggling when encountering educational challenges (Lowe and Cook, 2003). A major part of a student's academic self-efficacy or confidence to complete a task successfully (Bandura, 1997) is informed by self-reflection of previous performance and experiences (Elias and MacDonald, 2007). Educators cannot always impact previous experiences but can help to alleviate student fears and help students build confidence. Elias and Loomis (2000) suggest that multiple opportunities to be successful aid development of student self-efficacy. To counteract poor academic self-efficacy, educators should structure their courses to include and provide feedback on frequent low stakes assessments.

Low-stakes assessments increase academic self-efficacy by lowering stress. Students tend to see assignments and exams that are high stakes (a large proportion of their grade or major impact on future goals) as threatening (Putwain and Symes, 2014). The fear of failure and extreme negative consequences can move students to more performance-avoidance goals (for a review see Elliot and Church, 1997), where students are more concerned about performing worse than their peers rather than mastering material (Putwain and Symes, 2011). Performance-oriented achievement goals are more conducive to cheating as the fear of failure is stronger than the desire to understand the course content (Corrion et al., 2010). By providing frequent low-stakes assessments, educators can give students more frequent feedback, and frequent testing can help long-term retention (Karpicke and Roediger, 2007). This practice helps to strengthen students' academic self-efficacy by giving ample opportunities to learn from their previous experiences while also not putting too much pressure or focus on their performance. Instead, the focus in low-stakes assessment is learning, growth, and development.

EQUITY PEDAGOGY AS A SOLUTION TO FACTORS IMPACTING ACADEMIC MISCONDUCT CHOICES

Equity pedagogy is an integral part of promoting a culture of academic integrity through allowing instructors to meet students where they are despite the individual and environmental factors by which students from underrepresented backgrounds have been impacted (McGee Banks and Banks, 1995). In addition to establishing an environment that is inclusive of students from a variety of backgrounds, cultures, and experiences, equity pedagogy also diminishes positional inequities by encouraging students to be facilitators of their own learning rather than relying on instructors as "citadel[s] of knowledge" (McGee Banks and Banks, 1995, p. 153). Rather than attempting to memorize information, students are instead prompted to be generators of knowledge by presenting their perspectives and identifying multiple solutions to solve problems.

According to McGee Banks and Banks (1995), traditional testing and grading standards are also challenged under equity pedagogy, and frequent feedback is favored over standard grading mechanisms. Students are provided detailed feedback on their work which creates "opportunities for teachers to identify areas of competence as well as to suggest strategies for improvement and remediation" (p. 155). As it relates to academic integrity, equity pedagogy fosters learning that is inclusive and provides students with ownership over the acquisition, interrogation, use, and retention of knowledge. Ownership and inclusivity aid in relieving students from the pressure of high-stakes assessment that might normally lead to engagement in academic misconduct by scaffolding the content and coursework and promotes student choice, ownership, relevance, and utility as mentioned above. As a result, students are likely to be actively engaged in their learning process without the temptation of academic misconduct.

Culturally Responsive Teaching (CRT), which places a priority on integrating culture, ethnic identity, home experiences, and community into the educational experience of the student (Gay, 2018) is an example of a framework that can support equity pedagogy. CRT can increase utility and relevance of assignments through connection to more aspects of every student's life than are the basis for traditional coursework. Skillful application of CRT promotes academic integrity through motivating students to engage with course material given the increased opportunities to connect their lived experiences to course content (Schraw et al., 2007).

Ownership and inclusivity aid in relieving students from the pressure of high-stakes assessment that might normally lead to engagement in academic misconduct by scaffolding the content and coursework and promotes student choice, ownership, relevance, and utility as mentioned above. As a result, students are likely to be actively engaged in their learning process without the temptation of academic misconduct.

APPLYING PEDAGOGICAL SOLUTIONS: HIGH IMPACT PRACTICES

High Impact Practices (HIPs) provide a framework where the principles and strategies addressed above can be applied in ways that enhance the student learning experience (e.g. Diggs, 2021). Bertram Gallant (2017) outlined benefits of active learning pedagogies that decrease inclination toward academic misconduct and improve the student experience through organizing courses around learning goals, increasing student motivation, and presenting opportunities for students to engage in metacognition. The following sections outline examples of high impact pedagogical frameworks that include strategies to engage students in their own learning and decrease reasons why students would pursue unauthorized shortcuts. For each example, we provide an explanation of the practice, evidence for its effectiveness, and connections to strategies recommended more generally in the previous section for promoting academic integrity. Connections between HIPs and pedagogical strategies are listed in Table 1.

PROJECT-BASED LEARNING

Project-Based Learning (PjBL) allows students to apply course content, using knowledge, skills, and abilities, to complete a project that offers meaningful solutions to relevant questions (Lee et al., 2014). PjBL uses an inquiry process based in real-world issues and enhances the utility and relevance of course-work, a pedagogical solution known to increase performance (e.g. Hulleman et al., 2017). Learners work together to solve problems as they integrate, apply, and construct knowledge with instructors as facilitators who provide feedback and assistance throughout the project development and completion (Guo et al., 2020).

Studies have shown positive effects of PjBL on overall student achievement. In a meta-analysis of outcomes from PjBL in biology, physics, chemistry, and general science, Baleman and Keskin (2018) found that student academic performance in science courses was 86 percent higher in PjBL than through traditional teaching methods. Another meta-analysis showed a positive, medium- to large-sized statistical effect of the benefits on academic achievement through PjBL over traditional teaching across multiple academic disciplines (Chen and Yang, 2019).

Engagement with course content through the facilitative structure of projects promotes academic integrity in multiple ways. In terms of temptation and opportunity, specific structures used in project designs decrease likelihood that students can easily locate a project on the internet that meets the criteria for a given course. The progression of steps and scaffolding used to build makes each step more feasible and makes organizing time more manageable; builds student confidence, especially in those with skill gaps; and provides feedback opportunities to enhance clarity of expectations (Guo et al., 2020).

The high impact practice of PjBL is more likely to engage students due to the highly participatory role for students in project creation and realistic connections to real world and personal issues and problems. Given that faculty shift into a facilitative role, PjBL changes the dynamic of instructor as giver of information and student of receiver of information (Guo et al., 2020). Learning and applying content through projects also decreases direct assessment of facts that are easy for students to access from unauthorized sources and increases assessment of Higher Order Thinking Skills (HOTS) like application and critical thinking (Prananda et al., 2020). This shift can decrease performance pressure on students to always have the one correct answer and can increase the likelihood that students demonstrate content mastery through alternative forms of assessment. In PjBL, opportunities for showing mastery are particularly highlighted in the demand for content application.

SERVICE-LEARNING

Service-learning, also termed Community-Engaged Learning (Donohue and Plaxton-Moore, 2018), integrates community service with course learning goals through faculty and/or academic program leaders partnering with a community organization to design projects and activities that benefit the organization and provide "real world" and relevant application of course concepts. Important conditions of high-quality service-learning are that the service be meaningful, connected to course learning goals as a form of instruction, and processed through student reflection (Seifer and Connors, 2007).

Service-learning can engage students with multiple possibilities for application: teaching others, developing communication for outreach efforts, solving problems, conducting research, and other pursuits that enable students to deepen learning and apply course content to efforts that are beneficial to the community (Boise State University, 2021). Studies show benefits of quality service-learning for multiple stakeholders: course instructors, students, institutions, and community organizations (Salam et al., 2019). The following areas of demonstrated benefits from service-learning are those that can proactively decrease the likelihood that students may engage in academic misconduct:

1. **Attitudes toward self, including self-efficacy and awareness of students' own abilities** (Celio, 2011; Yorio and Ye, 2012): Service-learning presents opportunities for improvement and mastery in the ways students view their own strengths. This outcome area addresses lack of confidence and perception of skill gaps that can motivate students to engage in academic misconduct (Hattingh et al., 2020).

2. **Academic performance** (Celio et al., 2011; Yorio and Ye, 2012): Improvements in academic performance found in studies of service-learning outcomes decrease risk of academic misconduct, as Grade Point Averages (GPAs) have been shown to be negatively correlated with academic misconduct (McCabe et al., 2001).

3. **Attitudes toward school and learning, increased enjoyment of class, and overall academic engagement** (Celio et al., 2011): Service-learning has potential to mitigate the risk of misconduct that is present when students find that instructors are disengaged or that courses are disorganized (Anderman and Murdock, 2007).

4. **Civic engagement** (Celio et al., 2011) **and under-standing social issues** (Yorio and Ye, 2012): This area of outcomes from service-learning courses includes altruism and reported feelings of civic responsibility. Yu et al. (2017) found that a stronger level of "beyond-the-self focused purpose" (p. 418) and relevant engagement in co-curricular activities are both associated with lower levels of academic misconduct.

5. **Determination and persistence** (Yorio and Ye, 2012): Yorio and Ye (2012) reported that, across multiple studies, determination and persistence formed part of the higher order outcome characterized as personal insight from participation in service-learning. A top reason identified in Amigud and Lancaster's (2019) analysis of student requests for paid coursework services was inability to finish the work. Laziness and procrastination have been found to contribute to the time management issue that leads some students into academic misconduct (Hattingh et al., 2020).

Developing community partnerships and creating service-learning projects requires relationship building and continual reflection on instructor and student intentions to avoid some common pitfalls identified by Davis in 2006 assumptions by both instructors and students that service is simple and that it is always "good," both of which can easily lead to disregard for realities of structural inequity. One of the most important principles is that service-learning addresses actual needs expressed and framed through genuine collaboration with community partners (Honnet and Poulson, 1989 as cited by American Psychological Association, 2021).

The promise of Community-Engaged Learning for promotion of academic integrity comes with a caution for equity of those who participate and those who are community partners in service-learning. A major risk of service-learning projects is white saviorism, a tendency for privileged students to approach service as "saving" those who are deficient rather than understanding and being motivated by helping to transform without an implied hierarchy of worthiness (Cammarota, 2011). Everyone involved in a community partnership needs to learn about and reflect upon power structures and needs to be invested in addressing what is truly best for community partners.

To develop service-learning experiences that increase educational and engagement-related benefits and decrease risk of academic misconduct for all students, institutions need to avoid publicity that reinforces white savior narratives, such as the pattern of White students assisting young people of color in the majority of the photographs used on university websites (Donohue et al., 2015). Donohue et al. (2015) caution, "… [i]f service-learning is to draw upon the talents of students from diverse backgrounds and to engage students in the type of community work that might develop the knowledge, skills, commitment to engage with society's complex problems, then the images selected to represent those aims should be reflective of those intentions" (p. 34).

COURSE-BASED UNDERGRADUATE RESEARCH EXPERIENCES (CURES)

Research experiences for undergraduates as a high impact practice engages students in using research skills that apply content learned in courses (Kuh, 2008). Course-based Undergraduate

Research Experiences (CUREs) bring direct research experience to a wider group of students (Ing et al., 2020) than when select students work or volunteer in research laboratories. While typically implemented in traditional Science, Technology, Engineering, and Math (STEM) disciplines, CUREs have been used and evaluated in social sciences (Ruth et al., 2021) and are emerging in other disciplines such as English, Anthropology, and History (University of North Carolina, 2021) and Music Therapy (Dvorak et al., 2020). CUREs differ from traditional laboratory courses that are limited to instructor-designed "cookbook" lab exercises through involving hands-on practice of all stages of relevant systematic inquiry, discovery of new information, and iterative processes (Auchincloss et al., 2014).

In a systematic review of CURE outcomes, Dvorak et al. (2020) found gains in student learning, attitudes, and motivation about involvement in STEM and confidence about pursuing a career in science. Outside of traditional STEM courses, a study of CUREs in social sciences showed outcomes similar to those in traditional STEM fields (Ruth et al., 2021). A multi-year comparison of lecture grades between students who participated in CUREs at a Hispanic-Serving Institution (HSI) showed that students who participated in research experiences in their introductory biology course performed at statistically significantly higher levels than an equivalent comparison group of students who did not have those experiences (Ing et al., 2020). For underrepresented students, CUREs overcome multiple barriers to gaining research experience, such as the intimidation associated with and cultural capital required for contacting faculty members, difficulty finding research opportunities, and the lack of paid research opportunity for students who need to use time outside of class and homework sessions to earn money (Bangera and Brownell, 2014).

CUREs allow students to generate research questions and to engage in learning where the right answer is not the primary goal of the experiences (Auchincloss, 2014), which promotes motivation to create original work and utility of assignments. Research is done in steps (Ruth et al., 2021); the process lends itself well to a scaffolded set of lower-stakes assignments on which students get feedback to build to a full project. Categories of CURE outcomes identified by Dvorak et al. (2020) and Ruth et al. (2021) connect to ways that CUREs promote academic integrity and have powerful potential to overcome reasons that students engage in academic misconduct.

1. **Increased Course Content Knowledge** (Dvorak, 2020), **Understanding of Research Process and Research Skills** (Ruth, 2021)—The gains shown in course performance increased student comfort and confidence in the research process and improved research skills. When students achieve and when they can see the tangible growth in knowledge and skills needed for research, they close skill gaps and decrease stress and pressure, and this may decrease academic misconduct.

2. **Better Perceptions of Learning Experiences and Course Satisfaction; Improved Attitudes** (Dvorak, 2020)—In articles reviewed in Dvorak et al. (2020), outcomes indicated that students reported higher satisfaction and improved attitudes about courses that included CUREs. These types of

enhanced learning indicators diminish motivation for students to engage in academic misconduct with the perception of a negative learning experience as justification (Rettinger and Kramer, 2009) or reality (Devlin and Gray, 2007).

IMPLEMENTATION OF HIGH IMPACT PRACTICES (HIPS)

In addition to the examples provided in the previous section, other High Impact Practices (HIPs) demonstrate similar qualities: high levels of engagement, relevance, feedback, and active learning (Kuh, 2008). These qualities counter reasons students engage in academic misconduct and form pedagogical structures that promote academic integrity from the inside out. Introducing and integrating HIPs into curricula is challenging, however (Vaz, 2019). Typical resistance to implementation of HIPs includes the pressure faculty feel to cover a large body of content, student comfort in passive forms of learning, faculty and student inexperience with active learning, and negative prior experience with group projects and teamwork.

Concrete institutional support is necessary in the form of investment in faculty development, robust support through faculty development centers or other networks, communities of faculty and professional staff to support change, and clear assessment plans (Vaz, 2019). Underlying this is the need for an institutional culture shift because "[s]ustainable change requires more than policies and practices; it involves a shift in focus away from what faculty members do and say to what students do and learn" (Vaz, 2019, n.p.). An example of institutional support for HIPs is that many institutions have developed civic engagement centers led by professional staff members to support service-learning (Saltmarsh et al., 2015). It is well worth the institutional investment in faculty development to support HIPs as part of promoting a culture of integrity as opposed to time and effort expended on vigilance about cheating.

CONCLUSION

Students engage in academic misconduct for a multitude of reasons, some due to features of their educational environment and others due to their own personal characteristics (Rettinger and Kramer, 2009). These reasons are likely to influence each other. When a student with poor time management skills encounters a highly disorganized course and unresponsive instructor, for instance, this student can become easily frustrated and desperate, introducing the risk that an unauthorized shortcut becomes the "least bad" way for the student to submit coursework on time. The reasons for academic misconduct are rarely malicious (Devlin and Gray, 2007). Instead, there are many issues of inequity, various cultural differences, a wide range of influential environmental contexts, and other individual differences that explain why some students may copy material from the internet or engage in other prohibited academic behaviors (Strangfeld, 2019).

Educators need to take stock of the causes to reframe their motivations and actions around the symptoms. Despite findings that academic misconduct is frequent and that there are easily understood reasons behind it (McCabe et al., 2001), faculty and university staff have taken highly punitive and deficit-minded approaches to plagiarism and other forms of misconduct with frequent use of criminal language to describe even plagiarism that is likely to come out of skill gaps (Bertram Gallant, 2017;

Diamond, 2019; Bertram Gallant, 2008). Freire (2000) stated that "Leaders who do not act dialogically, but insist on imposing their decisions, do not organize the people—they manipulate them. They do not liberate, nor are they liberated: they oppress" (p. 178). In essence, those who do not allow a dialogue to occur suppress the ideas and experiences of others. Awareness of inequities is essential as both a mindset for every step of the learning process and as the starting point toward actions that can eliminate features of a student's educational experience that cause learning to be difficult and possibly traumatic. From larger issues, such as overall course design down to more specific actions like the tone and wording of communication with students, every aspect needs reconsideration to create an equitable learning experience for every student.

Many reasons students engage in academic misconduct can in fact be traced back to poor pedagogy and impractical expectations for student understanding of higher education culture. Simple changes in pedagogy can be implemented to motivate and support students creating more authentic and original work (Bertram Gallant, 2017). These include structuring assignments to be broken up into smaller meaningful pieces across the semester, providing ample low stakes assessments (Putwain and Symes, 2014), providing autonomy through choice in assignments (Hanewicz et al., 2017), and developing opportunities for students to feel connected and valued in the course through self-expression and personal relevance (Hulleman et al., 2010). Many of these elements can be combined in highly engaging frameworks identified as High Impact Practices (Kuh, 2008). With these combined approaches, educators can work to improve the learning experience for all students, bridge some of the inequity gap, and promote academic integrity as a core value in the educational process.

REFERENCES

Ambrose, S., Bridges, M. W., Lovett, M. C., DiPietro, M. and Norman, M. K. (2010). *How learning works: 7 research-based principles for smart teaching*. San Francisco, CA: Jossey-Bass.

American Psychological Association (2021). Service learning in psychology, June 2. Available at: **https://www.apa.org/education/undergrad/service-learning** (Accessed May 15, 2021).

Amigud, A. and Lancaster, T. (2019). '246 reasons to cheat: An analysis of students' reasons for seeking to outsource academic work', *Computers & Education, 134*, pp. 98–107.

Anderman, E. M. and Murdock, T. B. (2007). *Psychology of Academic Cheating*. Ebook.

Auchincloss, L. S., Laursen, S. L., Branchaw, J. L., Eagan, K., Graham, M., Hanauer, D. I., Lawrie, G., McLinn, C. M., Pelaez, N., Rowland, S., Towns, M., Trautmann, N. M., Varma-Nelson, P., Weston, T, and Dolan, E. L. (2014). 'Assessment of course-based undergraduate research experiences: A meeting report', *CBE-Life Sciences Education, 13,* pp. 29–40.

Bandura, A. (1997). 'Self-efficacy: Toward a unifying theory of behavioral change', *Psychological Review, 84*(2), pp. 191–215.

Bangera, G., and Brownell, S. E. (2014). 'Course-based undergraduate research experiences can make scientific research more inclusive', *CBE—Life Sciences Education, 13*(4), pp. 602–606.

Beasley, E. M. (2014). 'Students reported for cheating explain what they think would have stopped them', *Ethics & Behavior 24*(3), pp. 229–252.

Bennett, K. K., Behrendt, L. S. and Boothby, J. L. (2011). 'Instructor perceptions of plagiarism: are we finding common ground?', *Teaching of Psychology, 38*(1), pp. 29–35.

Bertram Gallant, T. (2008). *Academic integrity in the twenty-first century: A teaching and learning imperative.* Jossey-Bass.

Bertram Gallant, T. (2017). 'Academic Integrity as a Teaching & Learning Issue: From Theory to Practice', *Theory Into Practice, 56*(2), pp. 88–94.

Boise State University (2021). Examples of SL in STEM, 1 June. Available at: **https://www.boisestate.edu/servicelearning/ stem/sl-in-stem-examples/** (Accessed May 14, 2021).

Bluestein, S. A. (2015). 'Connecting student-faculty interaction to academic dishonesty', *Community College Journal of Research and Practice, 39*(2), pp. 179–191.

Brookfield, S. D. (2000). *The Skillful Teacher.* Jossey-Bass.

Carter, R. T. (2007). 'Racism and psychological and emotional injury: Recognizing and assessing race-based traumatic stress', *The Counseling Psychologist, 35*(1), pp. 13–105.

Carter, P. L. (2018). 'The multidimensional problems of educational inequality require multidimensional solutions', *Educational Studies, 54*(1), pp. 1–16.

Celio, C. I., Durlak, J. and Dymnicki, A. (2011). 'A meta-analysis of the impact of service-learning on students', *Journal of Experiential Education, 34*(2), pp. 164–181.

Chen, C. H. and Yang, Y. C. (2019). 'Revisiting the effects of project-based learning on students' academic achievement: A meta-analysis investigating moderators', *Educational Research Review, 26*, pp. 71–81.

Corrion, K., D'Arripe-Longueville, F., Chalabaev, A., Schiano-Lomoriello, S., Roussel, P. and Cury, F. (2010). 'Effect of implicit theories on judgement of cheating acceptability in physical education: The mediating role of achievement goals', *Journal of Sports Sciences, 28*(8), pp. 909–919.

Crook, C. and Nixon, E. (2021) 'How internet essay mill websites portray the student experience of higher education', *The Internet and Higher Education, 48,* p. 100775.

Davis, A. (2006). 'What we don't talk about when we don't talk about service'. In A. Davis and E. Lynn. (Eds). *The Civically Engaged Reader: A Diverse Collection of Short Provocative Readings on Civic Activity* (1st ed., pp. 148–154). Great Books Foundation.

Day, N. E., Hudson, D., Dobies, P. R. and Waris, R. (2011). 'Student or situation? Personality and classroom context as predictors of attitudes about business school cheating', *Social Psychology of Education, 14,* pp. 261–282

deNoyelles, A., Mannheimer Zydney, J. and Chen, B. (2014). 'Strategies for creating a community of inquiry through online asynchronous discussions', *Journal of Online Learning & Teaching, 10*(1), pp. 153–165.

Devlin, M. & Gray, K. (2007). 'In their own words: a qualitative study of the reasons Australian university students plagiarize', *Higher Education Research & Development, 26*(2), pp. 181–198.

Diamond, K. (2019). 'Rejecting the criminal narrative: Designing a plagiarism avoidance tutorial', *Journal of Electronic Resources Librarianship, 31*(4), pp. 232–240.

Diggs, S. N. (2021). 'Got HIPs? Making student engagement enhancement a core part of program development with high impact practices', *Teaching Public Administration.*

Doménech-Betoret, F., Abellán-Roselló, L. and Gómez-Artiga, A. (2017). 'Self-efficacy, satisfaction, and academic achievement: the mediator role of Students' expectancy-value beliefs', *Frontiers in Psychology, 8,* p. 1193.

Donahue, D. M. and Plaxton-Moore, S. (2018). *The student companion to community-engaged learning: What you need to know for transformative learning and real social change.* Stylus Publishing.

Dvorak, A. L., Davis, J. L., Bernard, G., Beveridge-Calvin, R., Monroe-Gulick, A., Thomas, P. and Forstot-Burke, C. (2020). 'Systematic review of course-based undergraduate research experiences: Implications for music therapy education', *Music Therapy Perspectives, 38*(2), pp. 126–134.

Eccles, J. (1983). 'Expectancies, values, and academic behaviors'. In J. T. Spence (Ed.), *Achievement and achievement motives: Psychological and sociological approaches* (pp. 75–146). W. H. Freeman.

Elias, S. M. and Loomis, R. J. (2000). 'Using an academic self-efficacy scale to address university major persistence', *Journal of College Student Development, 41*(4), pp. 450–454.

Elias, S. M. and MacDonald, S. (2007). 'Using past performance, proxy efficacy, and academic self-efficacy to predict college performance', *Journal of Applied Social Psychology, 37*(11), pp. 2518–2531.

Elliot, A. J. and Church, M. A. (1997). 'A hierarchical model of approach and avoidance achievement motivation', *Journal of Personality and Social Psychology, 72*(1), pp. 218–232.

Elliot, A. J. and Harackiewicz, J. M. (1996). 'Approach and avoidance achievement goals and intrinsic motivation: A mediational analysis', *Journal of Personality and Social Psychology, 70*(1), pp. 461–475.

Franklin, A. J., Boyd-Franklin, N. and Kelly, S. (2006). 'Racism and invisibility: Race-related stress, emotional abuse and psychological trauma for people of color', *Journal of Emotional Abuse, 6*(2/3), pp. 9–30.

Freire, P. (2000). *Pedagogy of the oppressed*. 30th anniversary ed. New York: Continuum.

Garza Mitchell, R. L. and Parnther, C. (2018). 'The shared responsibility for academic integrity education', *New Directions for Community Colleges, 183*, pp. 55–64.

Gay, G. (2018). *Culturally responsive teaching: Theory, research, and practice*. Teachers College Press.

Gershenson, S. and Papageorge, N. (2018). 'The power of teacher expectations: How racial bias hinders student attainment', *Education Next, 18*(1), pp. 64–71.

Greenberger, S., Holbeck, R., Steele, J. and Dyer, T. (2016). 'Plagiarism due to misunderstanding: Online instructor perceptions', *Journal of the Scholarship of Teaching and Learning, 16*(6), pp. 72–84.

Guibert, P. and Michaut, C. (2011) 'Le plagiat étudiant', *Education et Sociétés*, *2*(28), pp. 149–163.

Hammond, Z. (2016). *Culturally responsive teaching and the brain: Promoting authentic engagement and rigor among culturally and linguistically diverse students.* Corwin.

Hattingh, F., Buitendag, A. K. and Lall, M. (2020). 'Systematic literature review to identify and rank the most common reasons for plagiarism', *Proceedings of the 2020 InSITE Conference.*

Hayes, N. and Introna, L. D. (2005). 'Cultural values, plagiarism, and fairness: When plagiarism gets in the way of learning', *Ethics & Behavior, 15*(3), pp. 213–231.

Heddy, B. C. and Sinatra, G. M. (2013). 'Transforming misconceptions: Using transformative experience to promote positive affect and conceptual change in students learning about biological evolution', *Science Education, 97*(5), pp. 723–744.

Hudley, A. H. C., Mallinson, C. and Bucholtz, M. (2020). 'Toward racial justice in linguistics: Interdisciplinary insights into theorizing race in the discipline and diversifying the profession', *Language, 96*(4), e200–e235

Hulleman, C. S. and Harackiewicz, J. M. (2009). 'Promoting interest and performance in high school science classes', *Science, 326*(5958), 1410–1412.

Hulleman, C. S., Godes, O., Hendricks, B. L., & Harackiewicz, J. M. (2010). Enhancing interest and performance with utility value intervention. *Journal of Educational Psychology, 102*(4),880-895.

Hulleman, C. S., Kosovich, J. J., Barron, K. E. and Daniel, D. B. (2017). 'Making connections: Replicating and extending the utility value intervention in the classroom', *Journal of Educational Psychology, 109*(3), p. 387.

Ing, M., Burnette III, J. M., Azzam, T. and Wessler, S. R. (2020). 'Participation in a Course-Based Undergraduate Research Experience results in higher grades in the companion lecture course', *Educational Researcher*, doi:10.0013189X20968097.

Jensen, L. A., Arnett, J. J., Feldman, S. S. and Cauffman, E. (2002). 'It's wrong, but everybody does it: Academic dishonesty among high school and college students', *Contemporary Educational Psychology*, *27*(2), pp. 209–228.

Karpicke, J. D. and Roediger III, H. L. (2007). 'Repeated retrieval during learning is the key to long-term retention', *Journal of Memory and Language, 57*(2), pp. 151–162.

Kuh, G. D. (2008). 'High-impact educational practices: What they are, who has access to them, and why they matter', *Association of American Colleges and Universities, 14*(3), pp. 28–29.

Lowe, H. and Cook, A. (2003). 'Mind the gap: are students prepared for higher education?', *Journal of Further and Higher Education, 27*(1), pp. 53–76.

MacGregor, J. and Stuebs, M. (2012). 'To cheat or not to cheat: rationalizing academic impropriety', *Accounting Education 21*(3), pp. 265–287.

Magolda, M. B. B. and King, P. M. (2004). *Learning partnerships: Theory and models of practice to educate for self-authorship.* Stylus Publishing.

Mahon, J. (2019). *Successful Pedagogical Practices for First-Generation College Students* (Doctoral dissertation, Indiana University of Pennsylvania).

McCabe, D. L. and Pavela, G. (2004). 'Ten (updated) principles of academic integrity: How faculty can foster student honesty', *Change: The Magazine of Higher Learning, 36*(3), 10–15.

McCabe, D. L., Treviño, L. K. and Butterfield, K. D. (1999). 'Academic integrity in honor code and non-honor code environments: A qualitative investigation', *The Journal of Higher Education, 70*(2), pp. 211–234.

McCabe, D. L., Treviño, L. K. and Butterfield, K. D. (2001). 'Cheating in Academic Institutions: A Decade of Research', *Ethics & Behavior, 11*(3), pp. 219–232.

McGee, E. O. (2020). 'Interrogating structural racism in STEM higher education', *Educational Researcher, 49*(9), pp. 633–644.

References

McGee Banks, C.A. and Banks, J. (1995). 'Equity pedagogy: An essential component of multicultural education', *Theory Into Practice, 34*(3), pp. 152–158.

Merkel, W. (2021). 'Collage of confusion: An analysis of one university's multiple plagiarism policies', *System, 96*, p. 102399.

Miles, D. (2018). 'The growth mindset: Action and practice for educational leaders (Unpublished Thesis, Concordia University, St. Paul)'. Available at: **https://digitalcommons.csp.edu/cup_commons_grad_edd/211/** (Accessed April 20, 2021).

Mills, K. J. (2020). '"It's systemic": Environmental racial microaggressions experienced by Black undergraduates at a predominantly White institution', *Journal of Diversity in Higher Education, 13*(1), pp. 44–55.

Mintz, S. (2020). 'Who are our students?'. InsideHigherEd, 15 May. Available at: **https://www.insidehighered.com/blogs/higher-ed-gamma/who-are-our-students-0** (Accessed April 20, 2021).

Murdock, T. B. and Anderman, E. M. (2006). 'Motivational perspectives on student cheating: Toward an integrated model of academic dishonesty', *Educational Psychologist, 41*(3), pp. 129–145.

Murdock, T. B., Miller, A. D. and Goetzinger, A. (2007). 'Effects of classroom context on university students' judgments about cheating: Mediating and moderating processes', *Social Psychology of Education, 10*(2), pp. 141–169.

Murdock, T. B., Miller, A. and Kohlhardt, J. (2004). 'Effects of classroom context variables on high school students' judgments of the acceptability and likelihood of cheating', *Journal of Educational Psychology, 96*(4), p. 765.

Niemiec, C. P. and Ryan, R. M. (2009). 'Autonomy, competence, and relatedness in the classroom: Applying self-determination theory to educational practice', *Theory and Research in Education, 7*(2), pp. 133–144.

Palloff, R. and Pratt, K. (2003). *The virtual student. A profile and guide to working with online learners.* Jossey-Bass.

Pecorari, D. (2008). *Academic Writing and Plagiarism: A Linguistic Analysis*. Continuum.

Prananda, M. R., Proboningrum, D. I., Pratama, E. R. and Laksono, P. (2020). 'Improving higher order thinking skills (HOTS) with Project-Based Learning (PjBL) model assisted by geogebra', *Journal of Physics: Conference Series, 1467*(1), p. 012027.

Putwain, D. W. and Symes, W. (2011). 'Teachers' use of fear appeals in the mathematics classroom: Worrying or motivating students?', *British Journal of Educational Psychology, 81*(3), pp. 456–474.

Putwain, D. W. and Symes, W. (2014). 'The perceived value of maths and academic self-efficacy in the appraisal of fear appeals used prior to a high-stakes test as threatening or challenging', *Social Psychology of Education, 17*(2), pp. 229–248.

Rettinger, D. A. and Kramer, Y. (2009). 'Situational and personal causes of student cheating', *Research in Higher Education, 50*(3), pp. 293–313.

Rubie-Davies, C. M. (2010). 'Teacher expectations and perceptions of student attributes: Is there a relationship?', *British Journal of Educational Psychology, 80*(1), pp. 121–135.

Ruth, A., Brewis, A. and Sturtz Sreetharan, C. (2021). 'Effectiveness of social science research opportunities: a study of course-based undergraduate research experiences (CUREs)', *Teaching in Higher Education*, pp. 1–19.

Ryan, R. M. and Deci, E. L. (2017) *Self-Determination Theory: Basic psychological needs in motivation, development, and wellness*. Guilford.

Salam, M., Iskandar, D. N. A., Ibrahim, D. H. A. and Farooq, M. S. (2019). 'Service-learning in higher education: A systematic literature review', *Asia Pacific Education Review, 20*(4), pp. 573–593.

Saltmarsh, J., Janke, E. M. and Clayton, P. H. (2015). 'Transforming higher education through and for democratic civic engagement: A model for change', *Michigan Journal of Community Service Learning, 22*(1), pp. 122–127.

Schraw, G., Olafson, L., Kuch, F., Lehman, T. K., Lehman, S. and McCrudden, M. T. (2007). 'Interest and academic cheating'. In E. M. Anderman & T. B. Murdock (Eds), *Psychological perspectives on academic cheating*. Elsevier.

Schmelkin, L. P., Gilbert, K., Spencer, K. J., Pincus, H. S. and Silva, R. (2008). 'A multidimensional scaling of college students' perceptions of academic dishonesty', *The Journal of Higher Education, 79*(5), pp. 587–607.

Seifer, S. D. and Connors, K. (2007). Faculty toolkit for service-learning in higher education. *Scotts Valley, CA: National Service-Learning Clearinghouse*.

Smit, R. (2012). 'Towards a clearer understanding of student disadvantage in higher education: Problematising deficit thinking', *Higher Education Research & Development, 31*(3), pp. 369–380.

Sopcak, P. (2020). Restorative practices for academic integrity. International Center for Academic Integrity | Cultivating Integrity Worldwide. Available at: **https://www.academicintegrity.org/blog/restorative-practices-for-academic-integrity/** (Accessed February 19, 2021).

Sotola, L. K. and Crede, M. (2020). 'Regarding class quizzes: A meta-analytic synthesis of studies on the relationship between frequent low-stakes testing and class performance', *Educational Psychology Review, 3*(32), pp. 1–20.

Spinelli, C. G. (2008). 'Addressing the issue of cultural and linguistic diversity and assessment: Informal evaluation measures for English language learners', *Reading & Writing Quarterly, 24*(1), pp. 101–118.

Sterngold, A. (2004). 'Confronting plagiarism: How conventional teaching invites cyber-cheating', *Change: The Magazine of Higher Learning, 36*(3), 16–21.

Strangfeld, J. A. (2019). 'I just don't want to be judged: Cultural capital's impact on student plagiarism', *SAGE Open*.

University of North Carolina (2021) *CURE course listings,* 3 June. Available at: **https://qep.unc.edu/cure/course-listings/** (Accessed May 15, 2021).

Vaz, R. F. (2019). 'High impact practices work', 1 June. Available at: **https://www.insidehighered.com/views/2019/06/04/why-colleges-should-involve-more-students-high-impact-practices-opinion** (Accessed May 15, 2021).

Wigfield, A. and Eccles, J. S. (2002). 'The development of competence beliefs, expectancies for success, and achievement values from childhood through adolescence', *Development of Achievement Motivation*, pp. 91–120.

Yorio, P. L. and Ye, F. (2012). 'A meta-analysis on the effects of service-learning on the social, personal, and cognitive outcomes of learning', *Academy of Management Learning & Education, 11*(1), pp. 9–27.

Yu, H., Glanzer, P. L., Sriram, R., Johnson, B. R. and Moore, B. (2017). 'What contributes to college students' cheating? A study of individual factors', *Ethics & Behavior, 27*(5), pp. 401–422.

CHAPTER 7

Beyond *Doing* Integrity Online:
A Research Agenda for Authentic
Online Education

Douglas Harrison and Sharon Spencer

University of Maryland Global Campus

Though online education arguably went "mainstream" in the middle of the last decade (Kentnor, 2015), the rapid move to teaching online during the Covid-19 pandemic was when this modality went viral. At the height of the pandemic, over 1.6 billion students worldwide were enrolled in online courses (Devex, 2021); by some estimates, 97 percent of students pursuing an undergraduate degree in the US moved online in 2020 (Chen, 2021). Across the profession in higher education, perhaps the most dominant theme of this abrupt move has been a consistent concern that online education is more cheatable than learning in real life (IRL) (Allessio and Messinger, 2021; Lederman, 2020). This concern is not new. In 2010, Watson and Sottile found evidence that most students believe they and their peers were more likely to cheat in online courses than those IRL. Similarly, in 2003, Kidwell and Laurel found faculty more likely to assume that students in online courses were more engaged in academic misconduct with greater frequency than those in classrooms with IRL instruction. The intensification of these perceptions and attitudes tracked the sustained growth over time in the prevalence of online education. The rise of the "new cheating economy" (Wolverton, 2016), particularly the growing threat of contract cheating across all sectors and modalities of higher education (Lancaster, 2019), has also had an outsized, negative perceptual impact on online learning.

The pandemic transformed this longstanding belief about online learning and academic misconduct into something close to conventional wisdom within and beyond academe. In early 2021, evidence began to emerge of an increase in instances of online academic misconduct in higher education. Even though this increase was a statistical inevitability, given that the proportion of students learning in online courses in 2020 went from ~32 percent to nearly 100 percent (Chen, 2021), it was reported across trade publications, national newspapers, and local outlets alike as prima facie cause for concern about the relationship of the move to online learning and students' proclivity to cheat—a narrative framing the plausibility of which relies on the widespread givenness of a belief in an online-learning integrity gap (WSJ Noted, 2021; Wicentowski, 2021; Redden, 2021; Espinoza, 2021).

At the same time, the increased visibility of and attention to online learning has also brought into sharp relief its potential to increase access for students—especially new college majority populations (Kizilcec et al., 2021). Educational research into online teaching and learning consistently notes that the best practices in online instruction are powerful drivers for success among marginalized students (Ozogul, 2018). A more recent line of scholarly inquiry is establishing how these best practices are also the cornerstones of authentic education for all learners (Gay, 2018; Villalpando, 2012). So, while the uneven experiences of online education in the pandemic have entrenched negative perceptions of online learning (Fain, 2019; Linley, 2020), the mass migration to this modality also presents a fortuitous opportunity to displace those perceptions with more realistic, evidence-based frameworks that enhance and strengthen academic integrity rather than militating against it.

CONTEXTS AND DEFINITIONS

One positive, tertiary effect of the increase in the number of students learning online (National Center for Education Statistics, n.d.)—even before the Covid-19 pandemic—has been to highlight the difference between remote teaching and online education, terms that are commonly confused and widely assumed to be interchangeable. They are not. In our introduction to this chapter, we chose to use "online education" for initial ease of reference, but the distinction between remote teaching and online education is critical to establish at this juncture. Remote teaching uses "fully remote teaching solutions for instruction or education that would otherwise be delivered face-to-face or as blended or hybrid courses" (Hodges et al., 2020). The attempt to re-create IRL classroom experiences most commonly occurs through synchronous, expository instruction via cloud-based video conferencing platforms—"Zoom lectures," in the vernacular. In contrast, "online education is a distinctive educational architecture intentionally designed for virtual teaching, learning, and assessment, with technology tools strategically deployed for engagement and outcomes, as well as wraparound services that provide support throughout the online student life cycle" (Harrison, 2020). Online learning may take place synchronously, asynchronously, or some mix of both. It can be fully online or in hybrid formats (a mix of IRL and online teaching and learning). Learning can be self-paced (open entry, open exit), class-based and term-bound, or a mix of class-based and self-paced learning (Hodges et al., 2020; Means et al., 2014). In other words, all online learning is remote teaching, but not all remote teaching is online learning.

Differentiating these instructional modalities and formats is critical to understanding academic integrity in online education. True online education, as opposed to remote teaching, aims to construct active and engaged teaching and learning experiences aligned to authentic assessments. In turn, these types of online experiences "that are well-constructed and promote student empowerment and reflection are less inclined to experience instances of academic misconduct" (Goldman et al., 2021, p. 17). Put another way, the best way to stop cheating online—or IRL—is to "teach better" (Lederman, 2020). This position is not, unfortunately, a given way of thinking in higher education regardless of modality. One reason for this is the staying power of deficit-model concepts of academic integrity, especially in relation to attitudes and beliefs about online learning. Deficit-model approaches to academic integrity emphasize the policing of student behavior and the administration of legalistic adjudications to punish academic misconduct. This punitive and "bureaucratic culture fosters the pervasive assumption that when students misbehave or achieve poorly, they must be 'fixed' because the problem inheres in the students or their families, not in the social ecology of the school . . . or classroom" (Weiner, 2006, p. 42). Going back at least two decades, research consistently finds that faculty and students perceive cheating online to be easier than in IRL assessments (Allessio and Messinger, 2021; Harton et al., 2019; Ison, 2020; Newton, 2018). Yet the research on the prevalence of academic misconduct in online learning suggests that misconduct is no more likely in distance education (Beck, 2014; Grijalva et al., 2006; Watson and Sottile, 2010;) and may actually occur less frequently than in IRL (Stuber-McEwen et al., 2009; Harrison, 2020).

EDUCATIONAL INTEGRITY AND ONLINE LEARNING

What to make of this disconnect? One likely factor is entrenched resistance to and suspicion of online teaching and learning in much of higher education (Gratz and Looney, 2020). The shift away from direct, didactic, and expository teaching methods ("sage on the stage") toward more active, engaged, and facilitative approaches ("guide at the side") is not exclusive to online learning (Foster et al., 2016; Lim, 2016; Morrison, 2014). But these latter methods are the gold standard among researchers and practitioners in online education (Fujita, 2020), so much so that online learning has perhaps been the most powerful force in pedagogical and curricular innovation in higher education over the past 20 years (Bok, 2003; Picciano, 2017; Sener, 2012; Walberg and Twyman, 2013). We will treat this phenomenon more fully below. Here, online-learning innovations matter for their disruptive effect on the faculty experience. These disruptive innovations are ".... often viewed by faculty as difficult and unnecessary" (Gratz and Looney, 2020, p. 2; Kentnor, 2015). Means et al. (2014) gives the example of a faculty member who "took umbrage" with the idea that online learning "...could be more effective than conventional classroom teaching and insisted, 'I put my PowerPoint slides online and it didn't make any difference!'" (p. 7). In this view, online instruction only has value (if at all) when it replicates and minimally intrudes upon traditional classroom approaches. This is, of course, not online learning but remote teaching.

The shift to remote teaching also foregrounded the visibility of another pedagogical issue often debated among educators regardless of teaching modality: student learning assessment. The high-stakes forms of student learning assessment most common to remote teaching (exams, tests, and other similar evaluations) are correlated with higher instances of academic misconduct arising from a misalignment between the form of assessment and the mode of administration (Corrion et al., 2010; Martin, 2020). Online proctoring and other assessment security technologies attempt to correct for this misalignment, but their failure to provide the desired level of security shows that the problem with high-stakes assessment is more fundamental and rooted in its limitations as a meaningful measure of learning. Taken together, these factors may have a reinforcing effect on faculty perceptions and attitudes when the shortcomings of remote teaching are mistakenly attributed to the online-learning experience.

The disconnect, then, between the perception of online learning as a hot zone for academic misconduct and the reality of online education is not a matter of whether or to what extent online learning compromises academic integrity. Rather this division bespeaks competing methodologies, philosophies, and visions for what postsecondary education is and how it should be carried out (Kentnor, 2015). What we talk about when we talk about academic integrity online is fundamentally a question of *educational* integrity and of ensuring that education authentically fulfills the promise and potential of every student who wants to learn in any modality. Online learning theory and practice embrace a set of pedagogical approaches to educational integrity that prioritizes flexibility in assignment topics and formats, choices in texts and source materials, a focus on situational and applied learning, peer-to-peer co-construction of knowledge, and authentic assessment of learning (Dawson, 2020; Fujita, 2020; Means et al., 2014). In this model—regardless of modality—the educational experience is grounded in a collaborative rather than hierarchical relationships between faculty and student (Foster et al., 2016; Gratz and Looney, 2020; Morrison, 2014). All these components of online education may positively impact academic integrity because they are likely to increase the chances that students feel meaningfully connected to learning, that they are empowered to demonstrate what they know and have learned, that flexible responses to life pressures help minimize the risk of panic cheating, and that there is space for learning through failure. Drawing from the principles and practices of a growth-mindset approach (Dweck, 2007), many of the actions and behaviors that a deficit-mindset model would immediately identify as academic misconduct are instead treated in context through the "teachable moment" approach and other similar strategies (Bertram Gallant, 2017), especially the mishandling of sources and citations and failures to properly paraphrase. An in-context response reframes the student's position from offender to learner (Bertram Gallant 2008). It frees the faculty member from assuming legalistic and carceral postures (Weiner, 2006). Instead of faculty functioning primarily as graders on traditional assessments that measure knowledge at a fixed point in time and encourage students to learn superficially, in-context responses give students a meaningful role in shaping how they will demonstrate their knowledge in authentic assessments that show what they know. At the same time, these approaches allow faculty to inhabit the fullest conceptualization of the educator's role—to meet students where they are in order to help them realize the transformational potential of higher education.

WIDENING ACCESS TO AUTHENTIC LEARNING ONLINE

In these respects, the theory and practice of online education has helped enhance and sustain the kinds of robust institutional cultures of academic integrity that Bertram Gallant (2008) called for in challenging higher education to redirect the focus on integrity from "How do we stop students from cheating?" to "How do we ensure students are learning?" This latter question has received a particular inflection in online learning given the historically distinct profiles of online versus on-campus learners. The "classic distance education learners" are working adults (Williams, 2015; Xu and Jaggars, 2014) with family commitments, seeking to advance in or change their career (Fetzner, 2013; James et al., 2016; Newell, 2007; Romero and Usart, 2014). Many are active-duty military servicemembers or veterans (Molina and Morse, 2015). The formative phases of online learning in the late-twentieth and early twenty-first centuries were powerfully shaped by efforts to construct evidence-based teaching and learning experiences that would successfully serve this so-called continuing-education student population—what today is more commonly referred to as the new college majority. The universities that had the biggest shaping force in building the foundations of online learning in the US were either explicitly constituted to serve working-adult, military, and other under-served students or were invested in online learning within their professional-studies divisions where such students were dispro-portionately enrolled—most prominently at Western Gover-nors University, University of Maryland University College, the California Virtual College, and NYU Online (Kentor, 2015). Over the past decade, the rapid growth of online courses and programs across higher education has brought more traditional postsecondary student populations into the online learning environment. The percentage of students in US higher educa-tion taking at least one online course (a category of learner that is a serviceable proxy for a full-time, on-campus student) increased almost 10 percent between 2012 and 2018, from 26.1 percent to 35.3 percent, while the percentage of students who took no distance courses declined by roughly the same amount: from 73.9 percent in 2012, to 64.7 percent in 2018 (Hill, 2021).

These trends strongly suggest that what works for under-served, marginalized, and at-risk students—who were once the critical mass of online learners—works for everyone. There is both a need and opportunity within the scholarship of teaching and learning *and* the literature of academic integrity to validate the efficacy of curriculum development and instructional design in online learning for the increasingly diverse population of learners migrating to digitally distributed education. The online adult-learner population has proved to be a useful testing ground for pedagogical innovation, but these new ways of educating are highly translatable—and not even necessarily accurately labeled as "new." Early explorations into educating adults revealed a flipped script for the roles of educators and students. Knowles et al. (2020) notes that as early as 1926, conventional educational models required students to adjust to the curricular requirements set before them, but adult students demanded a curriculum built around their needs and interests as more independent critical thinkers. Over 50 years ago, Freire (2018) proposed building genuine partnerships and dialogues between students and educators to promote transformative learning rather than using traditional educational models that may fail to engage students fully in the why, what, and how of a curriculum. Students of all ages and backgrounds arguably benefit from customized curriculums and genuine partnerships with faculty members who encourage independent and critical thinking.

Given the skepticism about online learning among faculty, the building blocks for many online learning environments—including a disproportionate emphasis on pedagogical strategies and tactics to secure online assessments from cheating—may arise from many educators' defensive assumption that such approaches are necessary to compensate for a fundamental educational insufficiency of online learning. This is a fortuitous skepticism when it nevertheless results in a classroom that leverages technology in a variety of ways that are particularly suitable for online learning: collectively, these ways of using technology can form an approach that is distinct from traditional face-to-face classrooms but cohesive and comprehensive in its ability to meet students where they are.

The pandemic exponentially expanded data available to examine student perceptions of online learning and of academic integrity within the online classroom, but continuing misperceptions by researchers may muddy the waters despite the already extant and large data sets on which to base analyses.

Researchers in Thailand and Israel (Amzalag et al., 2021; Nagi and John, 2021), who focused on the impact of the recent surge in online learning, situated their research on academic integrity within the assumption that an increase in the use of technology facilitates unethical behavior. Data from these same studies indicate, however, that the reasons for engaging in academic misconduct were similar to pre-pandemic research—for instance, a lack of understanding of proper citation practices, assumptions that academic misconduct will not be identified or punished, lack of time, and pressure to meet requirements and attain a credential. Other research conducted prior to the pandemic (Spaulding, 2009; Swartz and Cole, 2013) indicates that many students do not, in fact, perceive the online learning environment as more conducive to cheating—a view that is perhaps based on students' increasing technical fluency, the ubiquity of open access to information online, and the convenience of online learning (Kilgour and Northcote, 2018).

DETERRENT TECHNOLOGY AND THE NEW CHEATING ECONOMY ONLINE

As the population of online students changes and expands, and as learner perceptions and acceptance of online learning grows, so too do efforts by educational institutions to guard against threats—real and perceived—to educational quality and academic integrity (Young, 2020). Beginning in the 2010s, "the cheating business" began to find commercial footing in a growing network of websites aggressively marketing a range of academically corrupt "services" to students in what Wolverton (2016) termed "the new cheating economy". The threats from the commercialization of academic corruption imperil the integrity and quality of higher education across all institution types, modalities, and student populations (Simonds and Gallagher, 2020). But for all the reasons we discuss above, the widespread assumption within and beyond higher education is that online learning is inherently more susceptible to these forces (Newton, 2020). Unsurprisingly, this frame of reference leads to a search for silver-bullet technologies that will vanquish the threats (Barthel, 2016; Newton, 2018). The pandemic supercharged this focus. A dramatic uptick in institutional adoption of remote proctoring software, browser-lockdown applications within learning management systems, and other software bolt-on tools testifies to the preoccupation with securing summative experiences in remote teaching environments (Flaherty, 2020). The widespread adoption of these tools met a swift backlash involving concerns about student privacy, data security, and the implicit bias that may be built into such technologies (Harwell, 2020; McKenzie, 2021). More deeply, the reflexive adoption of assessment-security technology and the desire for single-shot solutions point up a resistance to grappling with what all this means to sustain cultures of academic integrity. Why do so many students take advantage of, and why are so many others taken in by, the dark sides of the educational-services industry as part of the student-learning assessment process? Goldman et al. (2021) explored the idea that many of the conditions and situational factors driving students into the arms of the cheating economy arise at least in part from structural, systemic gaps within—and culturally non-responsive approaches to—curriculum, instruction, assessment, and student services. Wolverton (2016) glossed the spectrum of student-consumer personae propelling the growth of the new cheating economy as "first-years and transfers overwhelmed by the curriculum, international students with poor English skills, [and] lazy undergrads with easy access to a credit card" (para. 5). There is doubtless some truth in both perspectives. But new lines of reporting, research, and scholarly analysis are needed to move beyond the problem-admiration stage of fascinated outrage that still dominates much of academic discourse about the very real threats from commercialized corruption online.

ONLINE EDUCATION'S INNOVATIONS IN AUTHENTIC LEARNING

Examining why students cheat is critical not only to building and sustaining cultures of academic integrity but also in understanding how online learning might exacerbate those motivators. Two trans-modal motivators for cheating are students' lack of a sense of belonging to a learning community and an authentic connection with their instructor (Beasley, 2014; MacGregor and Stuebs, 2012). Because "students tend to internalize and accept values and practices as their own from contexts and communities where they feel connected" (Goldman et al., 2021, p. 14), classroom belonging can decrease the negative peer effects that drive unethical behavior (Carrell et al., 2005; Danner et al., 2007; Murdock et al, 2001; Stiggins, 2001). Relatedly, MacGregor and Stuebs (2011) found a correlation between perceptions that the instructor does not care about students and rationalization of cheating.

These dynamics are the lens through which we examine three primary domains of learning theory and practice for which online education has introduced important innovations: social presence, cognitive presence, and teaching presence. Why these three? There are many components to structuring an authentic online learning environment. First, as a larger framework, Picciano (2017) synthesizes research from analog distance-learning and online-educational theories to propose an integrated multimodal model for online education built on seven essential components:

- Content structured within a learning management system that leverages the uniquely powerful interactive modes of online engagement
- Social-emotional interaction via face-to-face teaching, tutoring, and advising—virtually, IRL, or blended
- Self-paced and other independently directed units of learning that might include the use adaptive learning technologies
- Dialectic and cooperative argumentation through synchronous and asynchronous discussions
- Assessment that uses learning analytics to improve curriculum, instruction, and customized feedback and support to students
- Peer collaboration and student-generated content through peer review and other peer-to-peer learning within wikis, multimedia presentations
- Reflection in journals, blogs, social media

Key to this model is an important foundational assumption: that online learning is not a subset or descendent of distance education but rather is one modality of teaching and learning in general—just as, for instance, we recognize high-impact practices as a constellation of modality-agnostic approaches deployed with responsiveness to the situational factors unique to a given learning environment (Linder and Mattison, 2018). Approaching online education as a subset of learning generally helpfully reframes innovations in online learning. Online learning innovations are both grounded in the specific, distinguishing contexts and features of teaching and learning online while also being translatable, relevant, and valuable to teaching and learning across modalities, sectors, institutions, and student populations in higher education. Another way to say this: everything in the bulleted list above is fully replicable in traditional learning environments IRL. More important for our purposes, the types of theories and methods that support the conditions, experiences, and outcomes associated with authentic education in an online modality substantively contribute to the profession's understanding of the principles and practices of academic integrity. Thus, our discussion in what follows of the concept and practice of multidimensional presence in online learning is a way of organizing three related networks of powerful pedagogical ideas and approaches in online learning and explicitly linking them to practices that enhance academic integrity across higher education.

Social Presence

The concept of presence plays a significant role in social constructivist accounts of teaching and learning articulated in modern educational theory by Vygotsky (1978) and in more recent literature (Knowles et al., 2015; Hammond, 2015). All learning—and the three interrelated operations of presence—occurs within the social system of the classroom (Wenger, 1998; Whiteside and Dikkers, 2014). IRL learning collapses physical and social presence so that they are experienced simultaneously in traditional classrooms. The physical proximity of learners and instructors brings with it a rich set of verbal and nonverbal pathways for students and faculty to get to know one another in the teaching and learning process through a host of interactions: small talk with classmates entering and leaving the classroom, the way the faculty member interacts with individuals and groups, an instructor's sense of humanness in lectures or lack of it, and so on. In the traditional classroom, all the educationally beneficial effects of learning environments with strong social presence can often seem or appear to happen organically: increased sense of belonging, lowered levels of loneliness and stress, and heightened levels of investment in the learning community (Whiteside, 2015).

Contrastingly, the remoteness of online learning means social presence must be intentionally cultivated and maintained. Hosler and Arend (2013) define social presence online as "one's ability, whether student or instructor, to project a human sensitivity, warmth and intimacy into an otherwise computer mediated environment, void of tonal, visual, and verbal cues found in the traditional classroom" (p. 149). The stakes for student success and academic integrity in all this are high. The sense of community and belonging that helps motivate students to learn and succeed authentically—and avoid panic cheating or the kind of rushed, sloppy work that can lapse into breaches of integrity—relies significantly on the instructor's ability to cultivate and sustain a strong social presence online. The approaches that support social presence are most consistently associated in the literature with constituent components of high-impact practices, communities of practice, and communities of inquiry (Kuh, 2005, Linder and Mattison, 2018; Pallof and Pratt,

2001). Few researchers (Murdock et al., 2007) have thoroughly explored how to cultivate and maintain a strong social presence as a prophylaxis for academic misconduct in online learning, territory that remains largely uncharted in the research.

Cognitive Presence

Cognitive presence emerged from early research into technology-mediated distance learning. Garrison et al. (2001) define cognitive presence as "the extent to which learners are able to construct and confirm meaning through sustained reflection and discourse in a critical community of inquiry" (p. 11). Over the past 20 years, the theoretical frameworks for understanding cognitive presence and their application to online learning have evolved through two main phases: first-phase research focused on creating conceptual schema for understanding how student presence is operationalized in online environments (Garrison et al., 2000). Second-phase research synthesized the foundational conceptual models of the early 2000s and joined them to a focus on practical strategies in the online classroom (Hosler and Arend, 2013). This research indicates that a lack of cognitive presence can lead to discussions and other exchanges among students and faculty online that feel superficial and inauthentic, leading students to dismiss these activities as "busywork" and decide that shortcuts are necessary or acceptable. Strategies that most effectively support students at whatever stage of cognitive engagement and development they learn, both within and across learning units (Hosler and Arend, 2013), are more likely to deeply engage students and encourage authentic learning, thereby discouraging unethical behavior.

Without meaningful social and cognitive presence, students are less likely to experience the learning environment as serious, valuable, and worthwhile (Kilgour and Northcote, 2018). Students may then look to alternative and questionable value systems outside the norms of academic integrity at moments of high-stakes assessment—either out of a sense of desperation or from ethical lassitude born of intellectual indifference. More research that explores how social and cognitive presence can disrupt the patterns and behaviors that are associated with academic misconduct can enhance and sustain cultures of ethicality and integrity.

Teaching Presence

The Practical Inquiry Model posits teaching presence as a third dimension of the educational experience that requires dedicated curation in online environments. Anderson et al. (2001) define teaching presence as "the design, facilitation, and direction of cognitive and social processes for the purpose of realizing personally meaningfully and educationally worthwhile learning outcomes" (p. 5). Early work on teaching presence focused on the need for online instructors to create socio-emotionally supportive environments—a focus driven by widespread skepticism that the loss of IRL classroom interactions could deliver successful student outcomes. In effect, this focus, while important, privileged social presence over cognitive presence and instructor engagement, all of which are necessary to strengthen academic integrity and act as a deterrent to academic misconduct. The more recent evolution of the literature on the practice of universal design and accessibility offers valuable insights into creating learning experiences that meet the widest possible array of learning backgrounds and assessment experiences that allow students to have a meaningful role in shaping how they will demonstrate their knowledge (CAST, 2018). In so doing, these strands of work reinforce the abiding connection of academic integrity and authentic online learning. Fully mobilizing all dimensions of teaching presence empowers instructors to form genuine bonds of human connection with students, to co-construct a learning environment in which a shared commitment to mutual accountability thrives, and to establish the pathways of communication that will lessen the chances that students feel they have no way out but cheating when they do not know how to succeed or when life happens. Moreover, approaching the development of social and cognitive presence from the perspective of an empowered teaching presence also demonstrates the value of not treating online pedagogy as a subset of teaching in general. It short-circuits the online cheatability conversation by replacing a focus on modality with a focus on how to teach and learn most effectively.

CONCLUSION

The literature of presence in online learning collectively demonstrates both the innovative thrust of online-learning theories and practices over time and the widespread applicability of the principles upon which the best practices of online learning are based. Like the literature of academic integrity, which is only a few decades older than online education, the scholarship of teaching and learning online has enjoyed considerable growth and diversification over its comparatively short lifespan (Means et al., 2014). One of the pleasures in the research and writing of this chapter was consistently finding so many concepts, practices, and values shared across the literature of integrity and the literature of online learning. Teaching better really *is* the way to promote integrity and disincentivize academic misconduct, and the mainstream of scholars and practitioners have worked hard to make this a central concern of these fields.

Yet the pleasure in consistently finding a shared focus on student learning in the literatures of academic integrity and online learning was tempered by an equally consistent frustration: These literatures rarely intersect or leverage one another's insights and methodologies to explicitly build out and onto the connections that in the current state only implicitly bind them. The questionable quality of much of the remote teaching necessitated by the Covid-19 pandemic has been a mixed blessing for the reputation of online learning generally and its reputation for ethical resilience specifically. But the pandemic has also undoubtedly created an opening for new lines of inquiry that may in turn have a positive, lasting impact on future lines of research. At the same time, the explosion of interest in, concern over, and fear about the integrity of online learning during the pandemic highlights the degree to which so much of what is assumed to be obvious or given relationships between academic integrity and online education is in fact not well researched, documented, or understood—if at all. Addressing these gaps in scholarship and action research will be crucial to ground understandings of academic integrity online in evidence-based frameworks. The pandemic-fueled intensity of the online cheatability debates will undoubtedly make it alluring to pursue work that tries to definitively settle this question. But the literatures of the past 30 years in both online learning and academic integrity consistently suggest this question is a deficit-model distraction.

Instead, the future directions for these literatures point toward a reconceptualization of this work away from *online learning* and *academic integrity* and toward research agendas for the study of *authentic education*. The best work from the constellation of scholarship addressed here is already implicitly embracing the idea that integrity is modality agnostic. The opportunity for the next generation of scholar-practitioners in these fields is to make the scholarship of authentic education an explicit starting point and an operative principle to understand how all modalities of teaching and learning, including online education, can extend the promise of higher education to all types of twenty-first century learners.

REFERENCES

Alessio, H. M. and Messinger, J. D. (2021). *Faculty and student perceptions of academic integrity in technology-assisted learning and testing.* Frontiers in Education, April 20.

Amzalag, M., Shapira, N. and Dolev, N. (2021). 'Two sides of the coin: Lack of academic integrity in exams during the corona pandemic, students' and lecturers' perceptions'. *Journal of Academic Ethics.*

Anderson, T., Rourke, L., Garrison, D. and Archer, W. (2001). 'Assessing Teaching Presence in a Computer Conferencing Context'. *Journal of Asynchronous Learning Networks, 5*(2), pp. 1–17.

Barthel, M. (2016). How to stop cheating in college. *The Atlantic,* April 20. Available at: **https://www.theatlantic.com/education/archive/2016/04/how-to-stop-cheating-in-college/479037/** (Accessed November 11, 2021).

Beasley, E. M. (2014). 'Students reported for cheating explain what they think would have stopped them', *Ethics & Behavior, 24*(3), pp. 229–252.

Beck, V. (2014). 'Testing a model to predict online cheating—much ado about nothing', *Active Learning in Higher Education, 15*(1), pp. 65–75.

Bertram Gallant, T. (2008). *Academic integrity in the twenty-first century: a teaching and learning imperative.* San Francisco: Jossey-Bass.

Bertram Gallant, T. (2017). 'Academic integrity as a teaching & learning issue: From theory to practice', *Theory Into Practice, 56*(2), pp. 88–94.

Bok, D. (2003). *Universities in the marketplace: The commercialization of higher education.* Princeton University Press.

CAST (2018). Universal design for learning guidelines version 2.2. **UDIguidelines.cast.org**. Retrieved from: **http:// udlguidelines.cast.org** (Accessed November 11, 2021).

Carrell, S. E., West, J. E. and Malmstrom, F. V. (2005). 'Peer effects in academic cheating', *SSRN*, November 3.

Chen, C. (2021). *Distance learning statistics and growth of online education in 2020.* Available at: Otter.ai. blog.otter.ai/distance-learning-statistics/?form=MY01SV&OCID=MY01SV (Accessed November 11, 2021).

Corrion, K., D'Arripe-Longueville, F., Chalabaev, A., Schiano-Lomoriello, S., Roussel, P. and Cury, F. (2010). 'Effect of implicit theories on judgement of cheating acceptability in physical education: The mediating role of achievement goals', *Journal of Sports Sciences, 28*(8), 909–919.

Danner, F., Anderman, L. H. and Anderman, E. M. (2007). 'Perceptions of classroom testing and sense of class belonging: Effects on cheating in high school', [Conference Session]. American Educational Research Association, Chicago, IL. Available at: **https://www. researchgate.net/publication/265594507_Perceptions_of_ classroom_testing_and_sense_of_class_belonging_Effects_ on_cheating_in_high_school** (Accessed November 11, 2021).

Dawson, P. (2020). *Defending assessment security in a digital world: Preventing e-cheating and supporting academic integrity in higher education.* Routledge.

Devex. (2021). *Q&A: How Covid-19 can help reshape access to higher education*, February 11. Available at: **https://www.devex.com/**

news/sponsored/q-a-how-covid-19-can-help-reshape-access-to-higher-education-99101 (Accessed November 11, 2021).

Dweck, C. (2007). *Mindset: The new psychology of success.* New York: Ballatine.

Espinoza, D. (2021). During the pandemic, a rise in cheating, college officials say. *Texas Standard,* May 6. Available at: **https://www.texasstandard.org/stories/during-the-pandemic-a-rise-in-cheating-college-officials-say/** (Accessed November 11, 2021).

Fain, P. (2019). Takedown of online education. *Inside Higher Ed.,* January 16. Available at: **https://www.insidehighered.com/digital-learning/article/2019/01/16/online-learning-fails-deliver-finds-report-aimed-discouraging** (Accessed November 11, 2021).

Fetzner, M. (2013). 'What do unsuccessful online students want us to know?', *Journal of Asynchronous Learning Networks, 17*(1), pp. 13–27. Retrieved from: **http://files.eric.ed.gov/fulltext/EJ1011376.pdf** (Accessed November 11, 2021) .

Flaherty, C. (2020). Big proctor. *Inside Higher Ed,* May 11. Available at: **https://www.insidehighered.com/news/2020/05/11/online-proctoring-surging-during-covid-19** (Accessed November 11, 2021).

Foster M. K., West B. and Bell-Angus B. (2016). 'Embracing your inner "guide on the side": Using neuroscience to shift the focus from teaching to learning', *Marketing Education Review, 26*(2), pp. 78–92.

Freire, P. (2018). *Pedagogy of the oppressed.* (50th ed.). Bloomsbury Publishing Inc.

Fujita, N. (2020). 'Transforming online teaching and learning: Towards learning design informed by information science and learning sciences', *Information and Learning Sciences, 121*(7/8), pp. 503–511.

Garrison, D. R., Anderson, T., and Archer, W. (2000). 'Critical thinking, cognitive presence, and computer conferencing in distance education', *American Journal of Distance Education. 15*(1), pp. 7–23.

Gay, G. (2018). *Culturally responsive teaching: Theory, research, and practice.* Teachers College Press.

Goldman, J., Carson, L. and Simonds, J. (2021). *It's in the pedagogy: Evidence-based practices to promote academic integrity.* Manuscript submitted for publication.

Gratz, E. and Looney, L. (2020). 'Faculty resistance to change: An examination of motivators and barriers to teaching online in higher education', *International Journal of Online Pedagogy and Course Design, 10*(1), pp. 1–14.

Grijalva, T., Kerkvliet, J. and Nowell, C. (2006). *Academic honesty and online courses.* ResearchGate. Available at: **https://www.researchgate.net/publication/228771121_Academic_honesty_and_online_courses** (Accessed November 11, 2021).

Hammond, Z. (2015). 'Culturally responsive teaching & the brain: Promoting authentic engagement and rigor among culturally and linguistically diverse students'. Corwin Press.

Harrison, D. (2020). 'Online education and authentic assessment', *Inside Higher Ed.*, April 29. Available at: **https://www.insidehighered.com/advice/2020/04/29/how-discourage-student-cheating-online-exams-opinion** (Accessed November 11, 2021).

Harton, H. C., Aladia, S., and Gordon, A. (2019). 'Faculty and student perceptions of cheating in online vs. traditional classes', *Online Journal of Distance Learning Administration, 22*(4).

Harwell, D. (2020). Mass school closures in the wake of the coronavirus are driving a new wave of student surveillance. *The Washington Post*, April 1. Available at: **https://www.washingtonpost.com/technology/2020/04/01/online-proctoring-college-exams-coronavirus/** (Accessed November 11, 2021).

Hill, P. (2021). 'US higher education enrollment trends by distance education type, 2012–2018', **PhilOnTech.com**. Availableat:**https://philonedtech.com/us-higher-education-enrollment-trends-by-distance-education-type-2012-2018/** (Accessed November 11, 2021).

Hodges, C., Moore, S., Lockee, B., Trust, T. and Bond, A. (2020). 'The difference between emergency remote teaching and online learning', *Educause Review*, March 27. Available at: **https://er.educause.edu/articles/2020/3/the-difference-between-emergency-remote-teaching-and-online-learning** (Accessed November 11, 2021).

Hosler, K. and Arend, B. (2013). 'Strategies and principles to develop cognitive presence in online discussions', *Educational communities of inquiry: Theoretical framework, research, and practice*. Hershey, PA: Information Science Reference, pp. 148–167. DOI: 10.4018/978-1-4666-2110-7.ch009

Ison, D. C. (2020). 'Detection of online contract cheating through stylometry: A pilot study', *Online Learning, 24*(2), pp. 142–165.

James, S., Swan, K. and Daston, C. (2016). 'Retention, progression and the taking of online courses', *Online Learning, 20*(2). Retrieved from: **https://onlinelearningconsortium.org/read/journal-issues/** (Accessed November 11, 2021).

Kentnor, H. (2015). 'Distance education and the evolution of online learning in the United States', *Curriculum and Teaching Dialogue, 17*(1&2), pp. 21–34. **https://digitalcommons.du.edu/law_facpub/24** (Accessed November 11, 2021).

Kidwell, L. A. and Laurel, J. P. (2003). 'Student reports and faculty perceptions of academic dishonesty', *Teaching Business Ethics, 7*(3), pp. 205–214.

Kilgour, P. and Northcote, M. (2018). 'Online learning in higher education: Comparing teacher and learner perspectives'. In T. Bastiaens (Ed.), *Proceedings of EdMedia: World Conference on*

Educational Media and Technology (pp. 2089–2099). Association for the Advancement of Computing in Education (AACE). Available at: **https://www.learntechlib.org/p/184450** (Accessed November 11, 2021).

Kizilcec, R. F., Makridis, C. A. and Sadowski, K. C. (2021,). *Pandemic response policies' democratizing effects on online learning.* Proceedings of the National Academy of Sciences of the United States of America, March 16. Available at: **https://www.pnas.org/content/118/11/e2026725118** (Accessed November 11, 2021).

Knowles, M. S., Holton III, E. F., Swanson, R. A. and Robinson, P. A. (2020). *The adult learner: The definitive classic in adult education and human resource development* (9th ed.). Routledge.

Kuh, G. D. (2005). *Student success in college: creating conditions that matter.* San Francisco: Jossey-Bass.

Lancaster, T. (2019). 'Social media enabled contract cheating', *Canadian Perspectives on Academic Integrity, 2*(2), pp. 7–24.

Lederman, D. (2020). 'Best way to stop cheating in online courses? "Teach better"'. *Inside Higher Ed.*, July 22 Available at: **https://www.insidehighered.com/digital-learning/article/2020/07/22/technology-best-way-stop-online-cheating-no-experts-say-better** (Accessed November 11, 2021).

Lim J. M. (2016). 'The relationship between successful completion and sequential movement in self-paced distance courses', *International Review of Research in Open and Distance Learning, 17*(1), pp. 159–179.

Linder, K. and Mattison, C. (2018). *High-impact practices in online education: Research and best practices.* Sterling: Stylus.

Linley, M. (2020). *Foundations for good practice: The student experience of online learning in Australian higher education during the COVID-19 pandemic.* Australian Government Tertiary Education Quality and Standards Agency. Available at: **https://eric.ed.gov/?id=ED610395** (Accessed November 11, 2021).

MacGregor, J. and Stuebs, M. (2011). 'To cheat or not to cheat: Rationalizing academic impropriety', *Accounting Education, 21*(3), pp. 265–287.

Martin, L. (2020). *Foundations for good practice: The student experience of online learning in Australian higher education during the COVID-19 pandemic.* Australian Government Tertiary Education Quality and Standards Agency. Available at: **https://eric.ed.gov/?id=ED610395** (Accessed November 11, 2021).

McKenzie, L. (2021). 'DePaul sued over online proctoring tool', *Inside Higher Ed*, March 11. Available at: **https://www.insidehighered.com/quicktakes/2021/03/11/depaul-sued-over-online-proctoring-tool** (Accessed November 11, 2021).

Means, B., Bakia, M. and Murphy, R. (2014). *Learning online: What research tells us about whether, when, and how.* Routledge.

Molina, D. and Morse, A. (2015). *Military-connected undergraduates: Exploring differences between national guard, reserve, active duty, and veterans in higher education.* American Council on Education and NASPA—Student Affairs Administrators in Higher Education. Available at: **https://www.acenet.edu/Documents/Military-Connected-Undergraduates.pdf** (Accessed November 11, 2021).

Morrison C. C. (2014). 'From "sage on the stage" to "guide on the side": A good start', *International Journal for the Scholarship of Teaching and Learning, 8*(1), pp. 1–15.

Murdock, T. B., Miller, A. D. and Goetzinger, A. (2007). 'Effects of classroom context on university students' judgments about cheating: Mediating and moderating processes', *Social Psychology of Education, 10*(2), pp. 141–169.

Nagi, K. and John, V. K. (2021). 'A study of attitudes towards plagiarism among Thai university students', *European Journal of Foreign Language Teaching, 5*(4), pp. 21–35.

National Center for Education Statistics (n.d.). *Fast Facts.* Retrieved June 25, 2021, from **https://nces.ed.gov/fastfacts/display.asp?id=80**

Newell, C. C. (2007). *Learner characteristics as predictors of online course completion among nontraditional technical college students* (Doctoral dissertation). Retrieved from **https://getd.libs.uga.edu/pdfs/ newell_chandler_c_200705_edd.pdf**

Newton, D. (2018). Bots strike back at college cheating. *Forbes*, November 30. Available at: **https://www.forbes.com/sites/ dereknewton/2018/11/30/bots-strike-back-at-college- cheating/** (Accessed November 11, 2021).

Newton, D. (2020). 'Another problem with shifting education online: A rise in cheating', *The Washington Post*, August 7. Available at: **https://www.washingtonpost.com/local/education/ another-problem-with-shifting-education-online-a- rise-in-cheating/2020/08/07/1284c9f6-d762-11ea-aff6- 220dd3a14741_story.html** (Accessed November 11, 2021).

Newton, P. M. (2018). *How common is commercial contract cheating in higher education and is it increasing? A systematic review*. Frontiers in Education, August 30.

Ozogul, G. (2018). 'Best practices in engaging online learners through active and experiential learning strategies', *Interdisciplinary Journal of Problem-Based Learning, 12*(1), March.

Palloff, R. M. and Pratt, K. (2011). *The excellent online instructor: Strategies for professional development*. Jossey-Bass.

Picciano, A. G. (2017). 'Theories and frameworks for online education: Seeking an integrated model', *Online Learning, 21*(3), pp. 166–190.

Redden, E. (2021). 'A spike in cheating since the move to remote?', *Inside Higher Ed*, February 5. Available at: **https://www .insidehighered.com/news/2021/02/05/study-finds- nearly-200-percent-jump-questions-submitted-chegg- after-start-pandemic** (Accessed November 11, 2021).

Romero, M. and Usart, M. (2014). 'The temporal perspective in higher education learners: Comparisons between online and onsite learning' *European Journal of Open, Distance and E-Learning, 17*(1), pp. 190–209.

Sener, J. (2012). *The seven futures of American education: Improving learning and teaching in a screen captured world.* CreateSpace.

Simonds, J. and Gallagher, G. (2020). 'Spectrum of threats to academic integrity', *WCET Frontiers.* Available at: **https://wcetfrontiers .org/2020/10/15/spectrum-of-threats-to-academic-integrity/** (Accessed November 11, 2021).

Spaulding, M. (2009). 'Perceptions of academic honesty in online vs. face-to-face classrooms', *Journal of Interactive Online Learning, 8*(3), 183–198.

Stiggins, R. J. (2001). *Student-involved classroom assessment* (3rd ed.). Upper Saddle River, NJ: Prentice Hall.

Stuber-McEwen, D., Wiseley, P. and Hoggatt, S. (2009). 'Point, click, and cheat: Frequency and type of academic dishonesty in the virtual classroom', *Online Journal of Distance Learning Administration, 12*(3), pp. 1–10.

Swartz, L. B. and Cole, M. T. (2013). 'Students' perception of academic integrity in online business education courses', *Journal of Business and Educational Leadership, 4*(1), pp. 102–112.

Villalpando, O. (2002). 'The impact of diversity and multiculturalism on all students: Findings from a national study', *NASPA Journal, 40*(1), pp. 124–144.

Vygotsky, L. S. (1978). *Mind and society: The development of higher mental processes.* Harvard University Press.

Walberg, H. J. and Twyman, J. S. (2013). 'Advances in online learning'. In M. Murphy, S. Redding and J. Twyman (Eds), *Handbook on innovations in learning* (pp. 165–178). Center on Innovations in Learning; Information Age Publishing. Available at: **http:// www.centeril.org/** (Accessed November 11, 2021).

Watson, G. and Sottile, J. (2010). 'Cheating in the digital age: Do students cheat more in online courses?', *Online Journal of Distance Learning Administration, 13*(1). Available at: **https://www .westga.edu/~distance/ojdla/spring131/watson131.html** (Accessed November 11, 2021).

Weiner, L. (2006). 'Challenging deficit thinking', *Educational Leadership, 64*(1), pp. 42–45. Available, at: **http://www.ascd.org/ASCD/pdf/journals/ed_lead/el200609_weiner.pdf** (Accessed November 11, 2021).

Wenger, E. (1998). *Communities of practice: Learning, meaning, and identity.* Cambridge University Press.

Whiteside, A. L. (2015). 'Introducing the social presence model to explore online and blended learning experiences', *Online Learning, 19*(2). Available at: **https://olj.onlinelearningconsortium.org/index.php/olj/article/view/453** (Accessed November 11, 2021).

Whiteside, A. L. and Dikkers, A. (2014). *The power of social presence for learning.* Educause. Available at: **https://er.educause.edu/articles/2014/5/the-power-of-social-presence-for-learning** (Accessed November 11, 2021).

Wicentowski, D. (2021). 'More students cheat during virtual learning, Missouri researchers find', *Riverfront Times*, May 3. Available at: **https://www.riverfronttimes.com/newsblog/2021/05/03/more-students-cheat-during-virtual-learning-missouri-researchers-find** (Accessed November 11, 2021).

Williams, K. (2015). *The impact that technology and social systems have on African American student enrollment growth in totally online, hybrid/blended online, and face-to-face undergraduate degree programs* (Doctoral dissertation). Available from ProQuest Dissertations and Theses database. (UMI No. 3707786)

Wolverton, B. (2016). 'The new cheating economy', *The Chronicle of Higher Education*, August 28. Available at: **https://www.chronicle.com/article/the-new-cheating-economy/** (Accessed November 11, 2021).

WSJ Noted (2021). *Students are cheating more during the pandemic*, May 12. Available at: **https://www.wsj.com/articles/students-are-cheating-more-during-the-pandemic-11620840447** (Accessed November 11, 2021).

REFERENCES

Xu, D. Jaggars, S. S. (2014). 'Performance gaps between online and face-to-face courses: Differences across types of students and academic subject areas', *Journal of Higher Education, 85*(5), pp. 633–659.

Young, J. R. (2020). *What colleges are doing to fight the 'contract cheating' industry*. EdSurge, January 30. Available at: **https://www .edsurge.com/news/2020-01-30-what-colleges-are-doing-to-fight-the-contract-cheating-industry** (Accessed November 11, 2021).

CHAPTER 8

Celebrating 30 Years of Research
on Academic Integrity: A Review of the
Most Influential Pieces

**Ann M. Rogerson[1], Tricia Bertram Gallant[2],
Courtney Cullen[3], and Robert T. Ives[4]**

[1]University of Wollongong

[2]University of California, San Diego

[3]University of Georgia

[4]University of Nevada, Reno

The origins of the contemporary academic integrity research and practice movement can be traced back to 1992 when the International Center for Academic Integrity (ICAI), then the Center for Academic Integrity (CAI), was formed in response to Don McCabe's findings that the majority of students across in US higher education institutions were regularly cheating (McCabe, 1992). Since that time, thousands of studies have been conducted, and articles, books, and book chapters have been written, all of which shine light on the academic misconduct problem and the possible solutions. To celebrate this research, ICAI published a Reader[1] to highlight the foundational articles and book chapters that should be read if new to the field. The first edition of the Reader was published in 2012 in honor of ICAI's twentieth anniversary, and the second was published in 2022 to honor the 30th anniversary.

The Reader pieces were chosen by members of ICAI—the practitioners and researchers who work every day in the field of academic integrity. The pieces chosen were considered those to have most influenced scholarship, research, and practice. In this chapter, we analyze the Reader to glean lessons for practice and research and to elucidate trends in the topics and research methods over the last 30 years.

After describing the process used to create the Reader, we delve into our review of the Reader, comparing the range of themes, methods, and approaches between the two editions. This approach is possible because, in both editions of the Reader, we used the same criteria to choose pieces for inclusion. We begin our comparison with the prevalent themes identified, followed by a discussion about methodological differences found in the pieces included in the two editions. Then we explore the scholarly works and issues that are missing from the Reader yet still relevant to understanding the full academic integrity picture. Finally, we end with suggesting ideas for further research into motivations, prevention, detection, intervention, and compliance, which are critical to ensuring learning and attributing authorship.

---

[1]See **https://academicintegrity.org/resources/academic-integrity-reader** for the full list of pieces in both editions, summaries of the pieces, as well as a write-up about the history of the formation of ICAI and the influence of Don McCabe and others.

THE CREATION OF THE ICAI READER

The ICAI Reader was established as a collection and bibliography of the most influential scholarly pieces published on the topic of academic integrity between 1992 and 2020. This collection provides a reading list for new practitioners and scholars entering the field while also providing trusted sources to others who are interested in research on academic integrity. To create the collection, ICAI members were invited to nominate pieces that they found particularly influential in their own practice or research. Next, ICAI members were solicited to serve as editors and reviewers for the Reader to both compile the list of possible pieces to include, as well as to conduct evaluations of those pieces and make final decisions about inclusion.

For the Reader's first and second editions, editors were instructed to find possible scholarly articles for inclusion by conducting a Google Scholar (**https://www.scholar.google.com**) search for a specific year using each of the following terms: academic integrity, academic dishonesty, academic honesty, cheating, and plagiarism. From those search results, editors narrowed their selection of pieces according to the following criteria: 1) scholarly sources only (i.e. journal articles or book chapters, not books[2]); 2) focus on academic integrity in education (rather than, say, business ethics); 3) number of Google citations or downloads/views from a publisher's website; 4) broad appeal (e.g. not specific to one school or one geographic area); or 5) editors' choice. For the latter criteria, editors were allowed to nominate pieces that perhaps did not meet the first

---

[2]We did not include full books in the Reader simply because of the scope of the project, however interested readers can visit the ICAI website for a list of recommended books.

four criteria but did greatly influence their practice, had been referenced in their own writings, enlightened their understanding of academic integrity research or practice, and/or influenced their own research direction or design.

Once the Editors' lists were complete, the Lead Editor assigned two Reviewers to each piece. Reviewers were instructed to read each assigned piece and evaluate it based on the following four criteria: 1) enhanced the literature/knowledge base; 2) appealed to a broad, international audience; 3) offered something new to the field (e.g. perspective, research methods) at the time of publication; and 4) was of excellent overall quality (e.g. in study design, methods, writing, literature review). Pieces were rated on a six-point scale from zero (0) = not an important addition to the Reader through to five (5) = should definitely be included in the Reader. Those pieces that ultimately scored at least four (4) out of five (5) in the evaluation were selected for inclusion.

At the end of this exhaustive process, 42 scholarly pieces were selected for the first edition, and 44 were selected for the second. To prepare this chapter, we used Leximancer, a text mining software (**https://www.leximancer.com/**), to uncover key themes as well as trends. First, we explore our interpretation of the themes, trends and developments in academic integrity research topics, then we look at the research methods, participant pools, and data analyses that were used to uncover those themes.

CONTENT THEMES

The focus of academic integrity research and writings has both stayed constant and shifted over the last 30 years. Authors and researchers have constantly been interested in better understanding student behaviors—what they are doing and how often they are doing it. However, the range of behaviors that have been studied have shifted from analog (e.g. exam cheating and plagiarism) to digital (e.g. contract cheating via online platforms like Twitter). Likewise, authors and researchers have been consistently interested in the ways in which institutions can and should address cheating, but this interest has expanded to include the ways in which national governments can and should be partnering with institutions to address cheating. In this section, we explore these constants and shifts, highlighting what we see as the most interesting and relevant to both future research and practice.

The first edition helped confirm academic integrity as a significant issue for education and institutions while establishing a baseline for measuring and analyzing problems associated with academic misconduct. McCabe and colleagues, authoring 13 of the 42 articles in the first edition, are obviously key to this. McCabe's surveys of tens of thousands of students served to establish that baseline of self-reported cheating rates, but his findings (e.g. McCabe and Treviño, 1993; McCabe, Treviño and Butterfield, 2002) on the influencers of academic misconduct (e.g. cultures of integrity, peer behaviors/norms, and integrity policies) also helped establish the paths of inquiry for subsequent academic integrity research. For example, Bertram Gallant and Drinan (2006) applied institutionalization theory to explain the process by which academic integrity policy becomes inculcated to an institution's culture. Stearns (2001) examined the influence of instructors and their behaviors on academic integrity, while Whitley and Keith-Spiegel (2001) used the existing knowledge base to spell out all of the programmatic elements that need to be implemented to create an integrity culture.

The second edition builds on some of the issues identified in the earlier edition while broadening the scope of educational integrity as a global concern that can be seriously undermined by technology and social media. Primarily, we see a shift from a heavy focus on plagiarism in the first edition to a concentration of focus on contract cheating in the second, with over one quarter of selected articles related to this issue. Other themes of interest are policy and legal perspectives and student motivational and behavioral factors.

It is notable that contract cheating does not appear at all in the first edition given that it was first defined in the 1992–2009 time period by Clarke and Lancaster (2006). While the topic lacked traction as a sufficiently significant issue of interest to be included in the first edition, 13 pieces focus on the topic in the second edition. And a number of these papers take the definition by Clarke and Lancaster (2006)—students outsourcing assessable work to external contractors—and build on it to include other actions by students such as sharing and trading materials and answers, using ghost writers and impersonators (Bretag et al., 2018). Bretag et al. (2018) also note that the majority of contract cheating happens not by a paid professional on behalf of a student but rather more normally by family and friends for free or favor.

The prediction that contract cheating would present greater challenges for upholding academic integrity (Walker and Townsley, 2012) has certainly come true. Two of the articles in the second collection examine a range of literature about contract cheating, one being a meta-analysis of the prevalence of contract cheating in recent literature (Curtis and Clare, 2017). The other was a systematic literature review related to the purchasing of assignments between 1978 and 2016 (Newton, 2018). These articles present evidence to suggest that the level of contract cheating is increasing, highlighting that research into the issue is of continuing importance, and also an urgent imperative so that we can understand more.

There are two additional studies on contract cheating worth mentioning. Amigud and Lancaster (2019, 2020) used discourse analysis of Twitter exchanges to enhance our understanding of how students interact with contract cheating services to purchase assessments. As a result, the authors suggest that life issues outside a students' control and poor time management and planning may influence a student's outsourcing requests.

Beyond the focus on contract cheating, some pieces in the second edition explored the antecedents of misconduct. Personality and motivational factors influencing cheating are particularly prevalent, including one study on goal setting and achievement (Van Yperen, Hamstra and van de Klauw, 2011), one on the Big Five personality traits (Giluk and Posthelthwaite, 2015) and one on student confidence at the commencement of studies (Newton, 2016). Other psychology-based perspectives examined students' justifications for cheating (Stephens, 2017; Simkin and McLeod, 2010). Continuing the work of Eisenberg (2004) in the first edition, these studies provide insights into why students choose to breach educational integrity policy and how they justify their actions to themselves and others.

Not surprisingly, given the importance of policy in practice, both editions of the Reader include pieces that explore academic integrity policies. In the first edition, there was a prominent focus on honor codes given McCabe's work. However, in a nod to McCabe and Treviño's (1993) finding that honor codes are not the only policy solution to creating cultures of integrity, other authors explored policy alternatives. Aaron (1992), as well as Bertram Gallant and Drinan (2006), surveyed administrators to determine if and how academic misconduct was being addressed at the tertiary level of education, while other authors (e.g. Bertram Gallant and Drinan, 2008; Cole and Kiss, 2000; Kibler, 1993; Whitley and Keith-Spiegel, 2001) used previous research to theorize about what should be done at the institutional level. Together, these pieces represent the beginning of a global shift from a stance of institutional denial of cheating to institutional accountability for academic integrity. Although each of these pieces have been influential in research and practice, Kibler's (1993) work to connect academic misconduct with student development theory deserves special note for helping shift institutional responses to cheating from being more punitive to being more educational and developmental.

In the second edition, we see several more pieces that dig into institutional policies through empirical research. Bretag et al. (2011) identified essential elements of effective academic integrity policy through an exhaustive review of institutional policies across Australian universities (Bretag et al., 2011). A later study compared academic integrity policies across the UK and Europe (Glendinning, 2014) to conclude that while the majority of institutions have policies, they are not applied in a consistent manner. As we learned in the first edition from McCabe's work, understanding of policies is a key determinant of student behaviors and thus inconsistency in the application of policy is detrimental to achieving a culture of academic integrity.

While a focus on institutional policies existed in both editions, the exploration of legal frameworks for addressing cheating appears in the second edition, no doubt influenced by the intense focus on contract cheating over the last 10 years. In particular, Draper and Newton (2017) examined potential legal approaches to legislating against contract cheating in the UK (Draper and Newton, 2017). However, Sutherland-Smith (2014) cautions us against taking a legal approach to plagiarism management and advises us instead to focus on teaching and learning rather than punishment. In recommendations and practice, most of the legal solutions being explored to tackle contract cheating are focused on the providers of the services rather than the students themselves (Draper and Newton, 2017), so it is possible to have both a legal response to contract cheating as well as an educational one.

The identification of articles of interest in the legal and policy domain are indicative that academic integrity extends beyond the boundaries of an institution and into the commercial sphere. While institutions can design and administer policy around academic integrity, they have no jurisdiction over commercial enterprises, which are regulated by local and national governments. Therefore, in order to truly mitigate the negative impact of the contract cheating industry on learning and educational quality, institutions need the support of legislators to, as a starting point, outlaw the commercial industry as well as their deceptive marketing strategies.

Despite the presence in both editions of pieces that explored policy and legal approaches to reducing or preventing cheating, there are few studies in either edition that examined interventions directed at students to change attitudes and behaviors. This is interesting considering that much of the talk in practice is about such interventions. There are pieces in the first edition that theorized about what could be done (Bertram Gallant and Drinan, 2008; Hutton, 2006; Whitley and Keith-Spiegel, 2001); however, in the second edition, there are pieces that empirically examine interventions. For example, Dee and Jacob (2012) conducted a field experiment to see if they could reduce plagiarism by increasing students' understanding through a tutorial. Elander et al. (201) evaluated an intervention designed to enhance student "authorial identity" and found that by increasing student writing self-efficacy, as well as their understanding of authorship, could be a successful strategy. Similarly, Perkins et al. (2020) examined whether a class in "academic English" could help reduce plagiarism. Plagiarism wasn't the only area of interest for intervention studies. Ellis et al. (2020) assessed the effectiveness of "authentic assessments" for reducing contract cheating, while Ives and Nehrkorn (2019) conducted a meta-analysis of the research on interventions to find that similarity detection can work, as can education, honor codes and proctoring. While this is a good start to increasing research on interventions, the findings are variable and more research must be conducted.

RESEARCH APPROACHES: TRENDS AND DEVELOPMENTS

The quantity of research and the diversity of researchers and authors investigating academic integrity (and it's opposite, academic misconduct which includes cheating and plagiarism) has expanded over the last 30 years. Consequently, the ways in which the research is undertaken deserves exploration as the chosen methods greatly influence what we know, do not know, and are continuing to learn. In this section, we will examine and compare the methods, participant pools, and data analyses used throughout the pieces in the Reader across the two periods of the first edition (1992–2009) and second edition (2010–2020).

Methods

The majority of works in the Reader applied quantitative methods. Surveys appear as a popular method of data collection, likely because they allow for voluntary participation and the anonymity of a survey might help with self-disclosure of cheating behaviors (even though social desirability bias is still an issue). In the first edition, the works by McCabe stand out as setting the stage for much of the other research that followed, including further survey collection and descriptive analysis by Davis and Ludvigson (1995), Nonis and Swift (2001), and Eisenberg (2004). Toward the latter years of the first edition, some additional correlation and regression studies using survey data appear, including those by Jordan (2001) and Passow et al. (2006).

In the second edition, a new trend appeared. A handful of studies analyzed data promoting the purchase, trade, or exchange of assessment content collected from electronic media sources, including Twitter (e.g. Amigud and Lancaster, 2019, 2020), Google searches (e.g. Lancaster, 2020; Neville, 2012), RSS feeds (e.g. Ellis et al., 2020), and internet-based contract cheating sites (Rowland et al, 2018). These data sources are not found in the first edition, representing an innovative approach to taking advantage of relatively new technology to investigate larger patterns of threats to academic integrity. The applications of these new data sources are all focused on aspects of contract cheating showing some promise of revealing broader social and cultural predictors, as well as relevant personal characteristics of those with a propensity for academic misconduct.

The utilization of qualitative methods for understanding academic misconduct is less common in the Reader. However, when used, plagiarism was a common topic explored in the first edition. Two studies, for example, utilized content analysis, one to analyze graduate student writing samples (Pecorari, 2003), and the other to analyze focus groups and interviews with first- and second-year American undergraduate students (Power, 2009). These two studies help readers understand how plagiarism is understood and experienced by students as a moral issue (Power, 2009) and how plagiarism may often be the result of an unintended action rather than a malicious practice (Pecorari, 2003). There are two other qualitative pieces of note in the first edition. One, by Bertram Gallant (2007), used a case study approach (including interviews, document analysis) to take a deep dive into the integrity culture creation process on one campus. Another, by Payne and Nantz (1994), used the "long interview" to explore with students a situation in which they perceived themselves to have cheated (or been tempted to cheat) and how they interpreted that situation as well as their reactions to it. These qualitative approaches were unique at that time and, unfortunately, remain in the minority as quantitative studies still dominate.

Having said that, there are also some qualitative studies in the second edition, and these also used some interesting approaches. For instance, Amigud and Lancaster (2019) used discourse analysis to assess the market demand for contract cheating, while Rowland et al. (2018) used categorical coding to better understand the marketing strategies used by contract cheating websites to attract students to their services. Qualitative elements are also included in five mixed methods studies in the second edition. The qualitative data in these studies included analyzing students' justifications for ratings of samples of plagiarism (Hu and Lei, 2012), conducting focus groups to identify changes in authorial identity related to an intervention (Elander et al., 2010) using discourse analysis to examine price variation and assignment demands for contract cheating based on Twitter messages (Amigud and Lancaster 2020) and employing semi-structured interviews to understand higher education approaches to academic integrity education (Sefcik, Striepe and Yorke, 2020).

Participant Samples

The pieces in the first edition focused primarily on college students in the US, which is not surprising given that, up until the early twenty-first century, the ICAI was known as the Center for Academic Integrity (CAI), a national organization that only focused on researching student academic integrity. The US-centric focus of the first edition, represents the research powerhouse that was Don McCabe, his collaborators, and other North American researchers he inspired. For context, the Asia Pacific Forum on Educational Integrity (APFEI) was established 11 years after CAI in 2003 (Bretag, 2015). The Academic Integrity Council of Ontario (AICO), the first academic integrity organization in Canada, was formed another five years later in 2008 (Ridgely, McKenzie and Miron, 2019). In addition, during the timeframe of the first edition, researchers in Australia and the UK were primarily focused on plagiarism rather than the broader academic integrity conversation, leading to the first International Plagiarism Conference held in the UK in 2004 (Bretag, 2015). It was not until the timeframe of the second edition that academic integrity researchers in UK/Europe formed the European Network for Academic Integrity in 2017 (**https://www.academicintegrity.eu/**).

While the main student population studied in the first edition was undergraduate students, there are two pieces that featured K-12 students (Eisenberg, 2004; Strom and Strom, 2007) and one that featured graduate students (Pecorari, 2003). There are also several pieces that assessed faculty views, including faculty commitment to integrity (e.g. McCabe et al., 2003) and investigations of faculty-student relationships for links to trust and cheating behaviors (e.g. Stearns, 2001). Administrative staff are also included in both quantitative and qualitative studies as related to academic integrity policy, creation, promotion, and institutionalization (e.g. Aaron, 1992; Betram Gallant 2007; Bertram Gallant and Drinan, 2006).

In the second edition, the focus continues to be on collegiate students, but it is far more international, including studies with populations from Europe, Africa, and Asia. The availability of technological or social media-based data may have played a part in this. One study, which compared student cohorts in the US and Israel, found that personality traits, staff attitudes, institutional policies and course type are better predictors of cheating behavior rather than socio-demographic variables (Peled et al., 2019). A further study found higher rates of contract cheating among students who are not native speakers of the dominant language and are struggling to understand or complete work (Bretag et al., 2018). Another study, although conducted in the US, found that searches for cheating and contract cheating services are more likely to originate from US counties with higher income inequality gaps (Neville, 2012), elucidating a possible growing equity gap in integrity behaviors. What is apparent from the second edition is that while there are a couple of papers that look at the influence of nationality or language groups (for example Hu and Lei, 2012; Pecorari and

Petric, 2014), there appears to be fewer investigations into socio-demographic factors related to academic integrity involving race and ethnicity, gender identity, and age. Whether the lack of these types of studies is due to the potential of establishing perceptual biases of aligning cheating behaviors to any particular socio-demographic group is unclear; however, it is likely to be a factor in how this type of data is collected, studied, and reported.

Data Analysis

A further legacy of Don McCabe may be the heavy focus in the first edition on the use of descriptive statistics to explore self-reported cheating rates and student perceptions of the issue. These studies were instrumental in establishing a baseline rate of self-reported student cheating and the extent to which factors—such as honor codes (McCabe and Treviño, 1993; McCabe et al., 2002), peer behaviors (McCabe et al., 2001a; McCabe et al., 2001b), faculty behaviors (McCabe, 1993), moral obligations and neutralizations (McCabe, 1992), and individual characteristics (McCabe and Treviño, 1996)—are associated with increased levels of self-reported cheating at tertiary institutions.

In comparison to the quantitative works in the first edition, which generally reported descriptive statistics, the quantitative works included in the second edition spanned a wider range of statistical analyses. This includes more complex statistical applications, such as: analysis of variance—ANOVAs (e.g. Curtis and Vardanega, 2016; Dee and Jacob, 2011; Elander et al., 2010; Shu, Gino and Bazerman, 2011), regression (e.g. Cronan, Mullins and Douglas, 2018; Rundle, Curtis and Clare, 2019), pathway analysis (e.g. Simkin and McLeod, 2010), factor analysis (e.g. Rundle, Curtis and Clare, 2019), structural equation modeling—SEM (e.g. Peled et al., 2019), and Rasch analysis (e.g. Ehrich et al., 2016).

The use of more complex statistical approaches may reflect the development of more nuanced understandings of the relationships between predictors of academic integrity—including motivations, contexts, and personality traits—and cheating behavior. They are also reflective of continuing approaches that sought to examine academic integrity perspectives from an "at distance relationship" which is facilitated by the collection of survey data that is usually anonymized, thereby encouraging students and staff to be more honest in their responses (e.g. Bretag et al., 2018). The use of survey data has progressed from the work of the first edition in quantifying the extent of the problem across student populations and the range of associated influences on academic misconduct. These studies have assisted the higher education sector in acknowledging that the issue of academic integrity is significant and ongoing.

OTHER CONSIDERATIONS

It is important to note that the Reader was created by practitioners and researchers who work in higher education in some capacity, which likely accounts for the focus on that particular education sector. However that the focus on higher education is also representative of the sector in which the majority of research into academic integrity has occurred to date. The search criteria, and background of the editors suggests that the works that comprise the ICAI Reader are not necessarily representative of all of the work being done in the field of academic integrity or work that influences the field of academic integrity.

The focus on academic integrity research in higher education also misses a large and influential piece of the puzzle—how practices and behaviors at the primary and second... levels influence what we see in college and university. n... man and colleagues (e.g. Anderman, 2007; Murdock and Anderman, 2006) have conducted much of that influential work, particularly around how students' motivational habits and orientations are formed early on and greatly impact how they engage in their learning and school work, with or without integrity. The absence of works studying primary or secondary education students is unfortunate and readers are encouraged to seek them out.

It is also recognized that educational integrity is a topic of interest across all academic disciplines and that articles on the topic, therefore, appear in a range of disciplinary focused journals. While these pieces may influence researchers and practitioners in their respective disciplines, they tend to have lower citation rates and, therefore, lack broader application across the sector, which accounts for their absence in the Reader. Their absence does not mean they are any less valuable in understanding and addressing educational integrity issues. In particular, readers interested in discipline-specific integrity issues, particularly those that prepare students for licensed professions (e.g. dentistry, law, medicine) through practical examinations, for example, would be well served by searching for articles in those disciplinary-focused journals.

Research innovations that can move the field forward should be celebrated. At the same time, there may be important perspectives on academic integrity that are not well-represented in Reader. For example, the studies based on electronic social media data (for example Neville, 2012; Amigud and Lancaster, 2019, 2020) are not able to offer detailed descriptions of the people who generated those data. When participant demographics are available, they are generally self-reports of traditional data like age, gender, first/dominant language, and educational background (for example Bretag et al., 2018; Ellis et al., 2020). In this way, students primarily remain the "subjects" of the research rather than as contributors who are involved in constructing and informing the research from design to implementation to analysis. Moving forward, if we want our research to really impact student practices, researchers should consider involving students in data generation and analysis by using a method known within the social sciences as "action research" (Ferrance, 2000).

We can also see a geographic focus in the Reader, with the majority having been conducted in Australia, the US, or the UK. While recognizing these countries as homes to large communities of academic integrity research and practice, it is worth noting that the Reader was restricted to English language scholarly pieces. Despite this limitation, a few studies in the second edition included perspectives from more than one country (for example Glendinning, 2014; Peled et al., 2019), and some addressed countries or situations where English is not the dominant language (for example Ehrich et al., 2016; Hu and Lei, 2012). This perhaps demonstrates a shift between editions that academic integrity is a global rather than local phenomenon. While it is not clear how the results from the three primarily English-speaking countries generalize to other settings, some of the findings do have broader applications that transcend submissions confined to English based assessments (for example Lines, 2016; Rogerson, 2017). We look forward to seeing an increasing amount of research conducted within other countries so we can learn the extent of generalizability.

In addition to the geographic imbalance of studies, the type of misconduct studied did not reflect the prevalence of different types of misconduct. About one-third of the studies in the second edition focused specifically on contract cheating, while another third focused on plagiarism. While a few other works addressed academic integrity more generally (for example Bretag et al., 2018) , very few looked at other specific types of misconduct, such as cheating on exams or cheating on assignments (for example Hylton, Levy and Dringus, 2016). This imbalance may reflect the view that plagiarism and contract cheating seem to continue to be the most confounding behaviors. Yet, largely due to McCabe's research, we have more evidence that the prevalence estimates of traditional cheating behaviors (whether on exams or assignments) and plagiarism are, in general, several times higher than the prevalence estimates for contract cheating. This may also reflect the evolution of how contracting is defined and where it is classified in the spectrum of cheating behaviors.

Despite the apparent growing concern for reducing the prevalence of academic misconduct in educational environments, only three intervention studies are represented in the second edition; though this is an increase from the first, it is still a small fraction of the total number of studies. The underrepresentation of intervention studies is also reflected in the larger academic integrity literature base (Ives and Nehrkorn, 2019). The underrepresentation may also be a consequence of those works not being highly cited or being significantly more difficult to receive ethics approval and carry out than the typical survey research. However, it does limit the ability to make causal inferences about the ways in which we can reduce cheating and plagiarism.

Related to the dearth of intervention and experimental studies is the absence of institutional data in the collection, with the exception of program descriptions (Sefcik, Striepe and Yorke, 2020). Institutional data could include valuable qualitative and quantitative information about academic integrity. For example, institutional data would include the frequency and types of cases that were referred for adjudication or other intervention. This would allow for the comparison of reporting frequency, issues related to assessment type, disciplinary trends, and the key times of the likelihood of misconduct occurring. A key consideration in progressing this type of reporting and analysis is enhancing the appetite for transparency and openness to accountability by educational institutions, as well as playing down the impact of this type of information on institutional reputations. It also requires that academic misconduct behaviors are consistently defined so that data sets can be compared in a meaningful and useful way. Nationally consistent definitions would be a starting point, international consistent definitions are a more difficult objective and will take some time to debate and achieve. While consistent definitions would provide a means of analyzing comparative data moving forward, it will make it challenging to conduct retrospective comparative analysis when the criteria for categorization of cases varies from jurisdiction to jurisdiction.

RESEARCH SUGGESTIONS FOR THE COMING DECADE

In the first edition, the scope of academic misconduct was heavily researched and described but largely focused on analog variations of the behavior. By the second edition, the studies expanded into investigating behaviors facilitated by technology.

The methods used by researchers are still overwhelmingly quantitative with information gathered almost exclusively through self-reported survey data and almost all exclusively collected on undergraduate students in the US, Canada, Australia, and the UK. Based on methods and populations studied over the last 30 years, there is a significant amount of research left to be done.

Thematically, there are opportunities to expand and highlight the application of academic research into disciplinary areas to better understand and address how misconduct appears or is evident in different assessment types preferred in various disciplines or subject areas. Understanding what is normal within a discipline is a key to understanding what is not normal and, therefore, should be examined through a lens of potential misconduct. Business students appear more frequently in the literature and the second edition is no different (Rogerson, 2017; Teixeria and Rocha, 2010), but as the data from studies, such as Bretag et al. (2018) demonstrate, the issue is also prevalent but not necessarily as easily recognized in other disciplines.

As there is little comparative evidence of the broader impact of assessment type on academic integrity in general (Ellis et al., 2020) this is a rich area to explore, particularly after educational shifts required due to responses to the Covid-19 pandemic. While it is acknowledged that there is no cheat proof assessment type, comparisons of assessments within and across jurisdictions would provide information to underpin future assessment and course design. Important to this type of activity is measurement so that the impact of changes can be plotted and evaluated to inform future practice.

With the introduction of formal legislation in some countries designed to combat contract cheating, a unique research situation presents itself where the impact of legislation on cheating behaviors and academic misconduct can be examined, particularly via technological and social media. The invasive nature of social media and the accompanying data gathering over the Internet and social media platforms also present opportunities to examine academic integrity issues through the evaluation of data analytics. Coupled with this is the analysis of cross-institutional data to assist with the identification of patterns, behaviors, and the success of intervention strategies. It will take a holistic approach by the sector to combat the technological threats.

Future research should extend the application of more complex investigations into academic integrity to better reflect the intrinsically complex nature of the topic. Researchers need to develop innovative and open access data sources and designs to facilitate addressing a wider range of questions related to academic integrity. These points are also reflected in Bretag's (2020) *Research Agenda for Academic Integrity* volume which posits a range of present and emerging threats as potential research opportunities to better understand educational integrity while considering global, language-based, technological, policy, and disciplinary perspectives.

The field should also extend its investigation of academic integrity outside of higher education. It is, perhaps, easier to survey and study undergraduate students than younger students, but academic integrity, or the lack thereof, is a societal concern and should not be constrained to institutions where study takes place over three to four years. Students bring their previous educational norms into higher education, and further research is required to determine how those norms are established while confirming their applicability to student decision-making behavior as it relates to academic misconduct. Academic integrity, rebranded as educational integrity, moves the field in the right direction because it encompasses scholars and teachers, researchers, publications, and, yes, students.

Broadening the scope of academic integrity to educational integrity, however, is just one step in the right direction. When considering where the studies into academic integrity have taken place to date, the current geographic scope of research into academic integrity to investigate the generalizability of findings in developed and predominantly English-speaking countries is too narrow. Global partnerships and collaborative efforts are needed to further the field of educational integrity. This raises another interesting point. Scholars should also focus attention on equity issues related to academic integrity—who is being researched, why, and what structures and biases are inhibiting or facilitating educational integrity today?

Finally, research must promote sustainable and equitable practice. Scholars are at a unique inflection point. They have the opportunity to build a larger and more rigorous research base to identify evidenced-based practices that improve academic integrity. Individual institutions may feel that by ignoring the problem and not acting with transparency means that they are safe from educational misconduct. They are not. By exploring extant institutional data, researchers can collaborate to build better practices that are in line with their values to teach, learn, and serve those seeking knowledge.

CONCLUSION

The last 30 years of research into academic integrity has taught us a great deal. Academic misconduct is a complex topic facing students and faculty globally. It also reveals the continuing and expanding interest in the field where new perspectives are explored to provide better understanding of trends and emerging issues identified by scholars across a range of disciplines. The papers in the second edition demonstrate that academic misconduct has broadened beyond plagiarism and exam cheating to contract cheating, a much more insidious behavior that threatens not just student learning but also the integrity of the entire educational enterprise.

The second edition is also released at a pivotal time for academic integrity. In the wake of the Covid-19 pandemic, educational integrity has been in the spotlight. Educational design, curricular requirements, and timely yet fair adjudication processes are catching the eyes of stakeholders everywhere. The opportunity for research, assessment, and intervention experiments is growing, and so is the interest for those outside of student academic misconduct practitioners. The third edition will be released in 2032, and the scope, scale, and growth of educational integrity will surely be reflected by the changes in the field and directions of future research.

REFERENCES[3]

Aaron, R. M. (1992). 'Student academic dishonesty: Are collegiate institutions addressing the issue?', *NASPA Journal*, Winter (2), pp. 107–113.★

Amigud, A. and Lancaster, T. (2019). '246 reasons to cheat: An analysis of students' reasons for seeking to outsource academic work', *Computers & Education, 134*, pp. 98–107.★★

---

[3]References appearing in the Reader first edition are annotated with a single.★
References appearing in the Reader second edition are annotated with a double.★★

Amigud, A. and Lancaster, T. (2020). 'I will pay someone to do my assignment: An analysis of market demand for contract cheating services on twitter', *Assessment & Evaluation in Higher Education*, *45*(4), pp. 541–553.★★

Anderman, E. M. (2007). 'The effects of personal, classroom, and school goal structures on academic cheating'. In E. M. Anderman and T. B. Murdock (Eds), *The Psychology Academic Cheating* (pp. 87–106). Elsevier.

Bertram Gallant, T. (2007). 'The complexity of integrity culture change: A case study of a liberal arts college', *The Review of Higher Education*, *30*(4), pp. 391–411.★

Bertram Gallant, T. (2017). 'Academic Integrity as a teaching & learning issue: From theory to practice', *Theory Into Practice*, *56*(2), pp. 88–94.★★

Bertram Gallant, T. and Drinan, P. (2006). 'Institutionalizing academic integrity: administrator perceptions and institutional actions', *NASPA Journal*, *43*(4), pp. 61–81.★

Bertram Gallant, T. and Drinan, P. (2008). 'Toward a Model of Academic Integrity Institutionalization: Informing Practice in Postsecondary Education', *Canadian Journal of Higher Education*, *38*(2), pp. 25–44.★

Bretag, T. (2015). 'Educational integrity in Australia'. In T. Bretag (Ed.), *The Handbook of Academic Integrity*, (pp. 1–13). Springer.

Bretag, T. (2020) *The Research Agenda for Academic Integrity*, Edward Elgar, Cheltenham, 205 pages.

Bretag, T., Harper, R., Burton, M., Ellis, C., Newton, P., Rozenberg, P., Saddiqui, S. and van Haeringen, K. (2018). 'Contract cheating: A survey of Australian university students', *Studies in Higher Education*, *44*(11), pp. 1837–1856.★★

Bretag, T., Mahmud, S., Wallace, M. J., Walker, R., James, C., Green, M., East, J., McGowan, U. and Patridge, L. (2011). 'Core elements of exemplary academic integrity policy in Australian higher education', *International Journal for Educational Integrity*, *7*(2), pp. 1–10.★★

Bretag, T., Mahmud, S., Wallace, M., Walker, R., McGowan, U., East, J., Green, M., Partridge, L. and James, C. J. S. i. H. E. (2014). '"Teach us how to do it properly!" An Australian academic integrity student survey', *Studies in Higher Education, 39*(7), pp. 1150–1169.★★

Clarke, R. and Lancaster, T. (2006). 'Eliminating the successor to plagiarism: Identifying the usage of contract cheating sites', *Proceedings of the Second International Plagiarism Conference*. Gateshead: United Kingdom.

Cole, S. and Kiss, E. (2000). 'What Can We Do about Student Cheating? About Campus', May–June, 5–12.★

Cronan, T. P., Mullins, J. K. and Douglas, D. E. (2018). 'Further understanding factors that explain freshman business students' academic integrity intention and behavior: Plagiarism and sharing homework', *Journal of Business Ethics, 147*(1), pp. 197–220.★★

Curtis, G. J. and Clare, J. (2017). 'How prevalent is contract cheating and to what extent are students repeat offenders?', *Journal of Academic Ethics, 15*(2), pp. 115–124.★★

Curtis, G. J. and Vardanega, L. (2016). 'Is plagiarism changing over time? A 10-year time-lag study with three points of measurement', *Higher Education Research & Development, 35*(6), pp. 1–13.★★

Davis, S. F. and Ludvigson, H. W. (1995). 'Additional data on academic dishonesty and a proposal for remediation', *Teaching of Psychology, 22*, pp. 119–122.★

Dee, T. S. and Jacob, B. A. (2012). 'Rational ignorance in education a field experiment in student plagiarism', *The Journal of Human Resources, 47*(2), pp. 397–434.★★

Draper, M. J. and Newton, P. M. (2017). 'A legal approach to tackling contract cheating?', *International Journal for Educational Integrity, 13*(1), p. 11.★★

Ehrich, J., Howard, S. J., Mu, C. and Bokosmaty, S. (2016). 'A comparison of Chinese and Australian university students' attitudes towards plagiarism', *Studies in Higher Education, 41*(2), pp. 231–246.★★

Eisenberg, J. (2004). 'To cheat or not to cheat: effects of moral perspective and situational variables on students' attitudes', *Journal of Moral Education, 33*(2), pp. 163–178.★

Elander, J., Pittam, G., Lusher, J., Fox, P. and Payne, N. (2010). 'Evaluation of an intervention to help students avoid unintentional plagiarism by improving their authorial identity', *Assessment & Evaluation in Higher Education, 35*(2), pp. 157–171.★★

Ellis, C., van Haeringen, K., Harper, R., Bretag, T., Zucker, I., McBride, S., Rozenberg, P., Newton, P. and Saddiqui, S. (2020). 'Does authentic assessment assure academic integrity? Evidence from contract cheating data', *Higher Education Research & Development, 39*(3), pp. 454–469.★★

Ferrance, E. (2000). 'Action Research'. LAB at Brown University. Available at: **https://www.brown.edu/academics/ education-alliance/sites/brown.edu.academics. education-alliance/files/publications/act_research.pdf** (Accessed: November 16, 2021).

Hu, G. and Lei, J. (2012). 'Investigating Chinese university students' knowledge of and attitudes toward plagiarism from an integrated perspective', *Language Learning, 62*(3), pp. 813–850.★★

Giluk, T. L. and Postlethwaite, B. E. (2015). 'Big Five personality and academic dishonesty: A meta-analytic review', *Personality and Individual Differences, 72*, pp. 59–67.★★

Glendinning, I. (2014). 'Responses to student plagiarism in higher education across Europe', *International Journal for Educational Integrity, 10*(1), pp. 1–17.★★

Hylton, K., Levy, Y. and Dringus, L. P. (2016). 'Utilizing webcam-based proctoring to deter misconduct in online exams', *Computers & Education, 92–93*, pp. 53–63.★★

Ives, B. and Nehrkorn, A. (2019). 'A research review: Post-secondary interventions to improve academic integrity'. In D. M. Velliaris (Ed.), *Prevention and Detection of Academic Misconduct in Higher Education* (pp. 39–62). IGI Global.★★

Jordon, A. E. (2001). 'College student cheating: The role of motivation, perceived norms, attitudes, and knowledge of institutional policy', *Ethics & Behavior, 11*, pp. 233–247.★

Kibler, W. L. (1993). 'A framework for addressing academic dishonesty from a student development perspective', *NASPA Journal, 31*(1), pp. 8–18.★

Lancaster, T. (2020). 'Academic discipline integration by contract cheating services and essay mills', *Journal of Academic Ethics, 18*(2), pp. 115–127.★★

Lines, L. (2016). 'Ghostwriters guaranteeing grades? The quality of online ghostwriting services available to tertiary students in Australia', *Teaching in Higher Education, 21*(8), pp. 889–914.★★

McCabe, D. L. (1992). 'The influence of situational ethics on cheating among college students', *Sociological Inquiry, 62*(3), pp. 365–374.★

McCabe, D. L. (1993). 'Faculty responses to academic dishonesty: The influence of honor codes', *Research in Higher Education, 34*(5), pp. 647658.★

McCabe, D. L. and Treviño, L. K. (1993). 'Academic dishonesty: Honor codes and other contextual influences', *The Journal of Postsecondary Education, 64*(5), pp. 522–538.★

McCabe, D. L. and Treviño, L. K. (1996). 'What we know about cheating in college: Longitudinal trends and recent developments', *Change*, January/February, pp. 29–33.★

McCabe, D. L. and Treviño, L. K. (2002). 'Honesty and honor codes', *Academe, 88*(1), pp. 37–41.★

McCabe, D. L., Treviño, L., K. and Butterfield, K. D. (2001a). 'Dishonesty in Academic Environments: The Influence of Peer Reporting Requirements', *The Journal of Higher Education, 72*(1), pp. 29–45.★

McCabe, D. L., Treviño, L., K. and Butterfield, K. D. (2001b). 'Cheating in academic institutions: A decade of research', *Ethics & Behavior, 11*(3), pp. 219–233.★

McCabe, D. L., Treviño, L. K. and Butterfield, K. D. (2002). 'Honor codes and other contextual influences on academic integrity:

A replication and extension to modified honor code settings', *Research in Higher Education*, *43*(3), pp. 357–378.★

McCabe, D. L., Butterfield, K. D. and Treviño, L. K (2003). 'Faculty & Academic Integrity: The Influence of Current Honor Codes and Past Honor Code Experiences', *Research in Higher Education*, *44*(3), pp. 367–385.

McCabe, D. L., Treviño, L. K. and Butterfield, K. D. (2012). *Cheating in College: Why Students Do It and What Educators Can Do About It*. John Hopkins University Press.

Murdock, T. B. and Anderman, E. M. (2006). 'Motivational perspectives on student cheating: toward an integrated model of academic dishonesty', *Educational Psychologist*, *41*(3), pp. 129–145.

Neville, L. (2012). 'Do economic equality and generalized trust inhibit academic dishonesty? Evidence from state-level search-engine queries', *Psychological Science*, *23*(4), pp. 339–345.★★

Newton, P. M. (2016). 'Academic integrity: A quantitative study of confidence and understanding in students at the start of their higher education', *Assessment & Evaluation in Higher Education*, *41*(3), pp. 482–497.★★

Newton, P. M. (2018). 'How common is commercial contract cheating in higher education and is it increasing? A systematic review', *Frontiers in Education*, *3*(67).★★

Nonis, S. and Swift, C. O. (2001). 'An examination of the relationship between academic dishonesty and workplace dishonesty: A multicampus investigation', *Journal of Education for Business*, November/December, pp. 60–76.★

Passow, H. J., Mayhew, M. J., Finelli, C. J., Harding, T. S. and Carpenter, D. D. (2006). 'Factors influencing engineering students' decisions to cheat by type of assessment', *Research in Higher Education*, *47*(6), pp. 643–684.★

Payne, S. L. and Nantz, K. S. (1994). 'Social accounts and metaphors about cheating', *College Teaching*, *42*, pp. 90–96.★

Pecorari, D. (2003). 'Good and Original: Plagiarism and Patchwriting in Academic Second-Language Writing', *Journal of Second Language Writing, 12*(4), pp. 317–345.★

Pecorari, D. and Petrić, B. (2014). 'Plagiarism in second-language writing', *Language Teaching, 47*(3), pp. 269–302.★★

Peled, Y., Eshet, Y., Barczyk, C. and Grinautski, K. (2019). 'Predictors of academic dishonesty among undergraduate students in online and face-to-face courses', *Computers & Education, 131*, pp. 49–59.★★

Perkins, M., Gezgin, U. B. and Roe, J. (2020). 'Reducing plagiarism through academic misconduct education', *International Journal for Educational Integrity, 16*(1), p. 3.★★

Power, L. G. (2009). 'University students' perceptions of plagiarism', *The Journal of Higher Education, 80*(6), pp. 643–662.★

Ridgley, A., McKenzie, A. and Miron, J. (2019). Building a regional academic integrity network: Profiling the growth and action of the Academic Integrity Council of Ontario. Paper presented at the Canadian Symposium on Academic Integrity, Calgary, AB, Canada, April 18.

Rogerson, A. M. (2017). 'Detecting contract cheating in essay and report submissions: process, patterns, clues and conversations', *International Journal for Educational Integrity, 13*(1), pp. 1–10.★★

Rowland, S., Slade, C., Wong, K.-S. and Whiting, B. (2018). '"Just turn to us": The persuasive features of contract cheating websites', *Assessment & Evaluation in Higher Education, 43*(4), pp. 652–665.★★

Rundle, K., Curtis, G. J. and Clare, J. (2019). 'Why students do not engage in contract cheating', *Frontiers in Psychology, 10*(2229).★★

Sefcik, L., Striepe, M. and Yorke, J. (2020). 'Mapping the landscape of academic integrity education programs: what approaches are effective?', *Assessment & Evaluation in Higher Education, 45*(1), pp. 30–43.★★

Shu, L. L., Gino, F. and Bazerman, M. H. (2011). 'Dishonest deed, clear conscience: When cheating leads to moral disengagement and motivated forgetting', *Personality and Social Psychology Bulletin, 37*(3), pp. 330–349.★★

Simkin, M. G. and McLeod, A. (2010). 'Why do college students cheat?', *Journal of Business Ethics, 94*(3), pp. 441–453.★★

Stearns, S. A. (2001). 'The student-instructor relationship's effect on academic integrity', *Ethics & Behavior, 11*(3), pp. 275–285.★

Stephens, J. M. (2017). 'How to cheat and not feel guilty: Cognitive dissonance and its amelioration in the domain of academic dishonesty', *Theory Into Practice, 56*(2), pp. 111–120.★★

Strom, P. S. and Strom, R. D. (2007). 'Cheating in middle school and high school', *The Educational Forum, 71* (Winter), pp. 104–116.★

Sutherland-Smith, W. (2014). 'Legality, quality assurance and learning: competing discourses of plagiarism management in higher education', *Journal of Higher Education Policy and Management, 36*(1), pp. 29–42.★★

Teixeira, A. A. C. and Rocha, M. F. (2010). 'Cheating by economics and business undergraduate students: an exploratory international assessment', *Higher Education, 59*(6), pp. 663–701.★★

Van Yperen, N. W., Hamstra, M. R. W. and van der Klauw, M. (2011). 'To win, or not to lose, at any cost: The impact of achievement goals on cheating', *British Journal of Management, 22*(s1), pp. S5–S15.★★

Walker, M. and Townley, C. (2012). 'Contract cheating: A new challenge for academic honesty?', *Journal of Academic Ethics, 10*(1), pp. 27–44.★★

Whitley, B. E., Jr. and Keith-Spiegel, P. (2001). 'Academic integrity as an institutional issue', *Ethics & Behavior, 11*(3), pp. 325–342.

CHAPTER 9

The Next 30 Years: Lessons Learned and Predictions about the Future

David A. Rettinger[1] and Tricia Bertram Gallant[2]

[1]University of Mary Washington

[2]University of California, San Diego

The past 30 years of research into academic integrity reflects the tremendous changes that have occurred within higher education during that time. Academic integrity, after all, is not a problem in and of itself but rather a bellwether of the fortunes of our field. The lessons learned from the research described in these pages have implications for scholars, students, faculty, and administrators. It is only by reflecting on these lessons and by embracing the changes required can we hope to achieve our goal of benefiting society through education.

Our first observation is that the wheel of technology has turned dramatically in the past three decades. Plagiarism is as old as text, of course, but advances in technology made it much easier to find, reformat, and repurpose the work of others. Prior to the mid 1980's, plagiarism still required a student to find an obscure source and manually retype content for submission. The inclusion of cut/copy/paste in 1983 into the Apple operating system (Shudel, 2020) dramatically simplified the process of plagiarism although finding sources was still a manual operation. However, by the early 90's (Borgman, 2010), students consistently had access to online databases of thousands of papers, making plagiarism completely electronic. In time, search engines made plagiarism very easy to do and hard to detect; the '90's could be characterized as the "golden age" of plagiarism. This, in turn, prompted the invention of products designed to detect and document similarities in computer programs (MOSS), and text (Google, Turnitin™), spelling the beginning of the end of plagiarism (as Curtis points out) as the dominant concern for those seeking to promote academic integrity.

Thus, the wheel of technology turned again in the mid-2000's, away from plagiarism and toward contract cheating. As Lancaster and Curtis, both point out, these behaviors are not new but are facilitated by the massive connectivity and anonymity of the internet. The wheel is beginning to turn again, with new products designed to detect changes in authorship and, therefore, highlight instances of contract cheating. However, Lancaster highlights new technological concerns, including machine-generated text that will supplant contract cheating in the future. Only by responding to this threat with all of the tools at our disposal can higher education maintain relevance in the future.

How must we respond to contract cheating? As we can see from history, a technological solution will never be sufficient, but it is necessary. Just as similarity detection engines have made plagiarism more difficult but far from impossible to perpetrate, tools to document contract cheating will continue to emerge. However, as with all technological solutions, they will be insufficient to tackle the problem of contract cheating, and so, changes to policy, practice, and communication about academic integrity will be necessary. Moreover, new ways to circumvent assignment rules will be introduced, and new technologies will emerge. It's a game of "whac-a-mole," and institutions will always be catching up with the dishonesty industry. We must, therefore, expand our responses beyond the technological to the pedagogical.

This leads to a second set of observations, which is that we must consider academic integrity to be a "teaching and learning issue" (Bertram Gallant, 2017). To recover any loss we have experienced or perceived to have experienced in integrity over the last 30 years, we must first and foremost re-establish and refocus on the value and purpose of higher education. Our value and purpose cannot be found in issuing credentials but rather in facilitating, nurturing, and assessing the knowledge and learning that those credentials are meant to represent. In all of our focus on expanding access to higher education, increasing graduation rates, and establishing new sources of revenue, we have only reinforced for students that grades and degrees matter more than learning. And, in an era in which the opinions held by internet celebrities about serious social issues are trusted more than the knowledge of academic experts, it is understandable that students may not take the acquisition of knowledge seriously. Higher education must rebuild within our walls the value and purpose of learning but also reach beyond our walls to younger students, to policymakers, and to the general public to re-establish our credibility and utility in the modern world.

Academic integrity is also a teaching and learning issue because it is something that, itself, can be shaped, developed, and nurtured by the instructor and by classroom experiences. As Anderman, et al. point out, the antecedents of academic misconduct are formed early on in a students' educational experiences, while Waltzer and Dahl highlight that ethical behavior is an essential part of academic integrity and can be developed. Thus, higher education institutions should participate in reinforcing the lessons of academic integrity among younger students, teachers, and caregivers to encourage a growth mindset through a mastery orientation in our classrooms and in our homes. The foundation for academic integrity in higher education rests on enrolling students who are intrinsically motivated to develop mastery of material and who value the personal benefits of their efforts to learn. One concrete recommendation would be outreach to K-12 teacher training programs with the express purpose of reducing cheating by helping teachers create learning environments that are conducive to intrinsic motivation.

Once these students arrive at university, we must recognize that their experience will not necessarily be like that of students 30 years ago, and adapt our pedagogical approach accordingly. Our conception of who is "college material" has changed tremendously in recent years and so must our pedagogy. Goldman et al. highlight the importance of preparing students for higher education in a way that recognizes the diverse expectations and preparation that they bring with them. This must occur as they are onboarded throughout their education and in response to their mistakes.

Differences in background should be treated as a strength rather than a weakness. The "deficit mindset" that Harrison and

Spencer warn us about has created an adversarial and punitive approach to academic integrity that holds us back from meaningful change. Institutions and instructors must lean into differences to help students build community and create a consistent set of expectations woven from the varied strands of experience that students bring to their education. For example, Goldman et al. recommend providing more culturally responsive pedagogy so that students make connections between their academic work and those concepts that are most meaningful to them. A simple way to do this is to give students a choice of topics, and/or deliverables, or both when designing assessments.

As more students from around the world are able to attend post secondary education in the US, students' exposure to techniques of research, writing, and sourcing have become more varied. This creates a need and an opportunity to give students consistent training in these techniques. Goldman, Harrison and their colleagues provide examples that include explicit instruction on citation, paraphrasing, and the use of sources more generally. Beyond that, however, instructors must first consider the learning value in the assessments they choose e.g. is a research assignment the best or only option to demonstrate knowledge for each student? And then, once the assessments are purposefully chosen to meet the learning objectives, instructors must help students to see the purpose of them. It is no longer enough to assume that if a student has chosen our institution that their objectives or the ways in which they demonstrate knowledge and learning align with ours. Instead, we could engage our students in choices of learning assessments. Or when we don't, we must explicitly state the objectives of each assignment, course, and even educational program so that students may align their own goals with ours. In short, we must meet students where they are or provide them with a clear path to meet us. This does not imply that assessment or material must be simplified or "dumbed down", but rather that coursework must encourage students to develop the attitude that the work is relevant to their goals, the belief they can do the work, and they have the motivation to master the material. Assessments that are relevant can be *more* rigorous if students are engaged by them. Such a strategy may be particularly relevant for students who are marginalized or feel that they are because as Goldman et al. highlight, these strategies can also enhance inclusiveness.

Our final observation reflects a substantial move toward online education, the biggest change in higher education likely to occur in the next 30 years. As Harrison and Spencer point out, many of our students no longer "arrive" at university literally, but rather join remotely. This has many ramifications for teaching and learning, many of which will impact academic integrity. For example, academic integrity and misconduct behaviors have a social component, as Anderman et al. report, but social learning happens in different ways online than in person. Harrison et al. describe both the importance and challenges of making connections between students and faculty and among students. These connections become essential because they provide avenues for students to learn from one another about what is and is not appropriate behavior and create the accountability that can only come from genuine interpersonal trust.

Although academic misconduct is perceived as easier online, to some extent this reflects the difference between genuine online learning and remote teaching, which is often just in-person learning ported to the internet. The Covid-19 pandemic has solidified this belief among faculty and administrators who made a rapid move online that met with mixed results. True online learning, particularly assignments that are customized in real time are much harder to cheat on than static assignments that are revised on an annual (or even less frequent) basis. While no assignment may be "cheatproof," any change that raises the bar for misconduct while improving learning outcomes is a step in the right direction. In the next 30 years of research, we anticipate that online learning will continue to develop new pedagogical approaches that move farther away from the traditional in-person modes and toward tools that leverage technology. For example, a shift to dynamic learning systems that tailor learning experiences in real time to students' needs will take advantage of expert systems and machine learning tools. At the same time, a personalized learning experience will serve to reduce academic misconduct.

In conclusion, the past 30 years have shown that higher education is at a crossroads. Students and society are questioning the benefits, especially given rising costs, and this disillusionment is manifesting itself in many ways, including increasing academic misconduct. While some are quick to blame shifts in technology, it appears that changes in contract cheating are merely the latest version of an ongoing problem rather than a paradigm shift in academic integrity. The massive shift to online learning in response to the Covid-19 pandemic will continue into the future, and it represents an opportunity to reconsider the way we communicate our values to students and society at large and our priorities as we engage them in the important work of preparing for citizenship and professional life.

REFERENCES

Bertram Gallant, T. (2017). 'Academic Integrity as a Teaching and Learning Issue: From Theory to Practice', *Theory into Practice*, *56*(2), 88–94.

Borgman, C. L. (2010). *Scholarship in the digital age: Information, infrastructure, and the internet.* MIT Press.

Shudel, M. (2020). 'Larry Tesler, inventor of copy-and-paste computer functions, dies at 74'. *The Washington Post,* February 22. Available at: **https://www.washingtonpost.com/local/obituaries/larry-tesler-inventor-of-copy-and-paste-computer-functions-dies-at-74/2020/02/20/e5699f6e-541c-11ea-9e47-59804be1dcfb_story.html** (Accessed September 27, 2021).

Index

241

Index

INDEX